NIST 800-171 Made Simple

A Step-by-Step Compliance Guide for IT and Security Teams

Dr. Patrick Jones

OLYMPUS ACADEMY
PRESS

Table of Contents

Introduction to NIST 800-171

If you work in IT or cybersecurity and have ever come across a government contract, you've probably heard the term "NIST 800-171." And if you're like most professionals, you may have nodded, taken a note to look it up later, and then forgotten what it actually means.

This chapter is your chance to slow down, take a breath, and really understand what NIST 800-171 is all about—and why it matters so much to organizations like yours.

What Is NIST 800-171?

Let's start at the beginning. NIST stands for the *National Institute of Standards and Technology*. It's a U.S. government agency that, among many other things, publishes guidelines to help organizations manage their security and protect sensitive information. These publications are used in both the public and private sectors and are considered authoritative and trustworthy.

NIST Special Publication 800-171 is a specific set of guidelines that lays out how non-federal systems—like those in private companies—should handle something called Controlled Unclassified Information (CUI).

CUI is any information that the government wants to protect but that isn't classified. Think of engineering drawings, legal documents, or logistics plans. These may not be top secret, but in the wrong hands, they could cause problems.

So, if your company works with government data—maybe you're a contractor for the Department of Defense (DoD), NASA, or another federal agency—you're expected to keep that data secure. That's where NIST 800-171 comes in.

Why Does This Matter?

It's simple: If you don't follow NIST 800-171, you could lose your contracts. Or worse, you could suffer a security breach, expose sensitive government information, and face legal or financial consequences. Compliance isn't just a checkbox—it's a signal that your organization can be trusted with important information.

But it goes deeper than just meeting requirements. Implementing the recommendations in NIST 800-171 can actually make your entire business more secure. These controls cover everything from who can access your systems to how you monitor for suspicious activity. Following them helps build a strong foundation for cybersecurity—something every organization needs today.

Who Needs to Comply?

If your company handles CUI in any form, you're in scope. This includes:

- Government contractors and subcontractors
- Manufacturers in the defense industrial base (DIB)
- Educational institutions with federal research contracts
- Managed service providers supporting those organizations

Even if you're not directly dealing with the government but are part of a supply chain that does, you may be asked to demonstrate compliance. And with the rollout of CMMC (Cybersecurity Maturity Model Certification), the pressure is only increasing.

What Does Compliance Actually Look Like?

NIST 800-171 is structured around 14 control families. These are categories like:

- Access Control
- Audit and Accountability
- Configuration Management
- Media Protection
- System and Information Integrity

Each control family contains specific requirements—110 in total. They're designed to work together as a framework, making sure your organization is prepared to prevent, detect, and respond to cybersecurity threats.

At first glance, this might sound overwhelming. One hundred and ten requirements? Fourteen categories? It's a lot to take in.

But here's the good news: you don't have to do it all at once, and this book will break each part down into manageable, understandable pieces. You'll see how the controls relate to your actual environment—your users, your networks, your endpoints—and how to implement them using real-world tools and methods, especially within platforms like Microsoft 365, Entra, Intune, and Azure.

Why NIST 800-171 Is Not Just Another Framework

You might be wondering how this differs from other frameworks like ISO 27001, CIS Controls, or even NIST's own 800-53.

The key difference is that NIST 800-171 is designed specifically for protecting CUI in non-federal systems. That makes it more focused, more relevant, and more tailored for small-to-mid-sized businesses trying to stay competitive in government contracting.

Where ISO might feel like a mile-wide, inch-deep guide, 800-171 is a detailed roadmap that gives you a clearer path toward compliance for a specific goal: keeping government data safe on your systems.

What's Coming in This Book

Here's what you can expect as we move forward:

- Plain-language explanations of each control family

- Implementation advice tailored to IT professionals

- Tips on using Microsoft tools to align with the requirements

- Real-world stories and case examples to make the concepts stick

- Checklists and planning templates to help you assess your own environment

Each chapter will focus on one control family, explain what it is, why it matters, and how to implement it using practical steps. Whether you're starting from scratch or reviewing your current security posture, this book is designed to help you take action confidently.

Let's Get Started

The path to NIST 800-171 compliance doesn't have to be a confusing maze. With the right mindset and guidance, it becomes a series of smart, strategic steps that not only protect your organization—but also open doors to bigger opportunities.

So, let's take that first step together.

In the next chapter, we'll dive into Controlled Unclassified Information (CUI)—what it is, how to recognize it, and why protecting it is at the heart of the entire standard.

Understanding Controlled Unclassified Information (CUI)

If there's one term that sits at the heart of NIST 800-171, it's CUI— Controlled Unclassified Information. But what does that really mean?

CUI isn't some obscure legal jargon. It's a practical label used to describe sensitive information that may not be classified, but still deserves protection. And for many organizations, recognizing and managing CUI correctly is the first—and often most confusing—step on the road to compliance.

This chapter is your guide to demystifying CUI: what it is, why it matters, where it shows up, and how it connects to everything else in the NIST 800-171 standard.

What Exactly Is CUI?

Let's start with a clear definition.

Controlled Unclassified Information is information the U.S. federal government creates or owns that isn't classified but still needs to be protected when it's shared outside the government. Think of it as *sensitive, but not secret.*

Here's the key: just because something isn't labeled "Top Secret" doesn't mean it's okay to post it online or leave it unguarded in a cloud folder. Some data, even without being classified, can cause harm if mishandled—whether it's personal details about employees, design specs for military equipment, or financial records tied to government contracts.

The government doesn't want that kind of information misused, leaked, or falling into the wrong hands. That's where the CUI designation comes in. It's a way to flag certain types of data as requiring extra care—even if it's not under lock and key like classified material.

A Brief History of CUI

The idea of CUI might sound new, but it was actually created to clean up a long-standing problem.

Before 2010, U.S. government agencies used dozens of different labels to describe sensitive but unclassified data. One agency might call something "FOUO" (For Official Use Only), another used "SBU" (Sensitive But Unclassified), and yet another had their own custom markings. There was no consistency.

This patchwork of terminology created confusion—not just inside the government, but especially for private contractors working with multiple agencies. How do you know what to protect if everyone's using different labels?

To solve this, the government issued Executive Order 13556, which formally created the CUI Program. This program centralized and standardized how agencies handle sensitive data and defined a single, uniform system for categorizing and protecting it.

The National Archives and Records Administration (NARA) was put in charge of the CUI Program. They maintain the official CUI Registry, which lists all the recognized categories and their associated handling rules.

Real-World Examples of CUI

To make this more concrete, let's look at some real examples of what could be considered CUI:

- Engineering designs for aircraft parts used in Department of Defense contracts

- Technical data about software source code developed for a federal agency

- Personally identifiable information (PII) about military personnel

- Export-controlled documents subject to ITAR or EAR regulations
- Infrastructure blueprints for utilities or transportation networks
- Procurement schedules and contract pricing for government bids

If your company works in any of these areas, there's a good chance you've already handled CUI—whether you realized it or not.

And here's the tricky part: CUI isn't always clearly marked. That's why one of the most important skills in protecting CUI is learning to recognize it in the wild, even if it doesn't have a big red "CUI" stamp on it.

How Do You Know If You Have CUI?

Let's face it—this is the question that trips up a lot of organizations. You want to do the right thing, but you're not sure if what you're handling even qualifies as CUI.

There are a few ways to identify it:

1. Contractual Language
   If you're working under a federal contract, look for terms like "CUI," "sensitive data," or references to NIST 800-171 in the contract clauses. If the contract says you'll be receiving or generating CUI, then that data is in scope.

2. Markings and Labels
   In some cases, the data will be clearly marked. You might see labels like "CUI," "Controlled," or "DoD CUI" on documents or file headers. These are obvious signs that the information requires protection.

3. Communication from Agencies
   Government customers may verbally or in writing inform you that a dataset or file includes CUI—even if it's not marked.

4. Type of Information
   Even without markings, certain types of information should raise a flag. Does the data include PII, export-controlled information, legal findings, or anything that could harm national interest if leaked? If so, treat it like CUI until proven otherwise.

CUI Categories: One Size Does Not Fit All

One of the most misunderstood things about CUI is that it's not just one type of data. In fact, NARA's CUI Registry currently defines over 20 major categories, each with subcategories and specific handling rules.

Here are a few of the major CUI categories you might encounter:

- Privacy – PII, health records, student data

- Defense – Military-related technical information

- Export Control – Subject to ITAR or EAR

- Financial – Budget data, banking information, tax records

- Law Enforcement – Investigative reports, criminal justice data

- Critical Infrastructure – Schematics for power grids or transportation hubs

- Proprietary Business Information – Trade secrets or confidential vendor data used in government projects

Not every business will handle all these categories, but even dealing with just *one* puts you under the umbrella of NIST 800-171.

That's why identifying your organization's specific exposure to CUI is so important—it informs how you implement the required controls.

The Link Between CUI and NIST 800-171

Here's where the dots connect.

Once CUI leaves a federal agency and enters your systems—whether through an email, a contract document, or a file share—it becomes your responsibility to protect it.

And that's exactly where NIST 800-171 comes into play.

The purpose of the NIST 800-171 standard is to provide clear, actionable security requirements for non-federal systems that store, process, or transmit CUI. In other words: if you've got CUI, this is the blueprint you follow to keep it safe.

It's worth noting that NIST 800-171 doesn't tell you *how* to meet the requirements—it tells you *what* needs to be done. The "how" is up to you, and it may vary depending on your environment, tools, and team size. That's where this book will help bridge the gap, offering guidance on implementation using modern platforms and practical IT solutions.

Why CUI Protection Matters—Beyond Compliance

It's easy to think of CUI compliance as just another regulation, another checklist, another set of hoops to jump through.

But the reality is, CUI protection is part of a bigger cybersecurity picture—one that reflects how we live and work in a world where sensitive data moves quickly, spreads easily, and is constantly under threat.

Whether it's ransomware, insider risk, or foreign espionage, the threats are real. By implementing protections for CUI, you're also:

- Reducing your risk of breaches and fines
- Showing customers and partners that you take security seriously
- Building trust with government agencies and primes
- Setting a strong foundation for broader frameworks like CMMC, ISO 27001, or even FedRAMP

In short, this isn't just about passing an audit. It's about protecting your organization and the information it's trusted to handle.

Summary: Know What You're Protecting

Controlled Unclassified Information may sound like a government term—and it is—but it has very real implications for your business.

CUI is the reason NIST 800-171 exists, and understanding what qualifies as CUI is the first real step toward building a secure and compliant environment. If you don't know what you're protecting, it's nearly impossible to put the right safeguards in place.

As we continue through this book, you'll gain clarity on the specific protections required, how to implement them, and how to document and manage your compliance efforts.

But always remember this:

CUI isn't just a label—it's a responsibility.

Coming Up Next

Now that you know what CUI is and why it matters, it's time to explore the structure of NIST 800-171 itself. In the next chapter, we'll break down the 14 control families that make up the backbone of the standard. You'll see how the requirements are grouped, how they interact, and where to begin building your compliance roadmap.

Let's take a high-level tour of the framework before diving into each section one by one.

Overview of the 14 Control Families in NIST 800-171

Now that you know what Controlled Unclassified Information (CUI) is and why it matters, the next logical step is understanding the structure of the NIST 800-171 framework. This chapter is your guided tour through the 14 control families—the heart of the standard.

Each family represents a core area of cybersecurity. You can think of them as categories that organize the 110 total requirements into manageable pieces. Some focus on technology, others on people or processes—but together, they form a holistic approach to protecting CUI in non-federal environments.

We're not diving deep into the controls just yet (that's coming soon), but this overview will give you a map of what's ahead. It's the "big picture" moment before we get into the step-by-step work.

Why Control Families?

Before we get into each one, it's worth understanding *why* the framework is broken into control families at all.

Cybersecurity isn't a single action—it's a system of interconnected safeguards. One area, like access control, affects others, like incident response or system auditing. The 14 families help you group and manage related requirements without treating each of the 110 controls like a standalone checklist item.

This also makes it easier to assign responsibility: your IT team might handle system configurations, while HR and leadership handle personnel security. Each family can be approached with the right people, tools, and focus.

The 14 Control Families – High-Level Summary

Let's walk through each family with a plain-language explanation of what it covers and why it matters.

1. Access Control (AC)

What it's about: Who can access your systems and data—and under what conditions.

This family covers permissions, account restrictions, and controls for limiting CUI access to only authorized users. Think of it as your first line of defense. If someone shouldn't be seeing a file, they shouldn't even be able to find it.

Examples include:

- Restricting access to systems based on job role
- Requiring multi-factor authentication
- Preventing unauthorized use of shared accounts

2. Awareness and Training (AT)

What it's about: Educating your people to recognize threats and act securely.

Even the best tools won't help if users don't know how to spot phishing or follow security protocols. This family ensures your staff understands their responsibility in protecting CUI.

Examples include:

- Annual security awareness training
- Phishing simulations and response training
- Documented training completion for employees

3. Audit and Accountability (AU)

What it's about: Tracking what happens in your systems and who did it.

Audit logs are the digital fingerprints of your environment. This family ensures you can detect, investigate, and respond to suspicious behavior or data misuse.

Examples include:

- Generating and storing security logs
- Assigning user accountability for system actions
- Reviewing logs for anomalies

4. Configuration Management (CM)

What it's about: Standardizing and securing system settings and changes.

If you don't know how your systems are configured, it's hard to know if something's wrong. This family keeps your IT environment consistent, secure, and easier to manage.

Examples include:

- Using baseline images for system builds
- Disabling unnecessary services or ports
- Change control procedures for updates

5. Identification and Authentication (IA)

What it's about: Verifying users before they gain access.

This family ensures that only the right people—and devices—can connect to your systems. It's about strong passwords, identity validation, and secure logins.

Examples include:

- Requiring complex passwords
- Enforcing MFA
- Verifying devices before granting access

6. Incident Response (IR)

What it's about: Being prepared when something goes wrong.

No system is perfect. Incident response planning helps you respond quickly and effectively to security breaches or suspicious activity.

Examples include:

- Having an incident response plan
- Assigning roles during a security event
- Documenting and reporting incidents

7. Maintenance (MA)

What it's about: Securely maintaining systems—whether on-site or remotely.

System maintenance needs to be safe, documented, and controlled. This family addresses how updates and repairs are handled, especially when third-party vendors are involved.

Examples include:

- Approving and logging all maintenance activity
- Restricting remote maintenance tools
- Preventing unauthorized changes

8. Media Protection (MP)

What it's about: Securing physical and digital storage devices.

This family ensures that anything holding CUI—USB drives, hard disks, printed documents—is protected, tracked, and disposed of securely.

Examples include:

- Encrypting removable drives
- Controlling physical access to backups
- Shredding or wiping devices before disposal

9. Personnel Security (PS)

What it's about: Vetting and managing people who handle sensitive data.

Security isn't just about technology. This family ensures that individuals who can access CUI are trustworthy and that their access is removed when they leave.

Examples include:

- Conducting background checks
- Removing system access after employment ends
- Managing insider threat risks

10. Physical Protection (PE)

What it's about: Controlling physical access to systems and devices.

Your data might be in the cloud, but your laptops, servers, and Wi-Fi routers still exist in the real world. This family covers locks, badges, visitor logs, and secure areas.

Examples include:

- Locking server rooms

- Using cameras and access cards
- Escorting visitors around sensitive areas

11. Risk Assessment (RA)

What it's about: Identifying and prioritizing risks to your systems.

Risk assessments help you focus your efforts on the areas that matter most. This family ensures you're evaluating threats and acting accordingly.

Examples include:

- Performing periodic risk assessments
- Identifying new vulnerabilities
- Prioritizing security improvements based on risk level

12. Security Assessment (CA)

What it's about: Reviewing your security controls to see if they actually work.

It's not enough to set up controls—you have to test them. This family ensures that your policies and tools are being evaluated and improved over time.

Examples include:

- Conducting internal security audits
- Tracking remediation actions
- Updating documentation based on test results

13. System and Communications Protection (SC)

What it's about: Securing how systems talk to each other and how data moves.

This family handles encryption, segmentation, and ensuring your systems don't leak information through weak communication channels.

Examples include:

- Encrypting CUI in transit and at rest
- Isolating sensitive systems
- Blocking untrusted connections

14. System and Information Integrity (SI)

What it's about: Keeping systems accurate, up-to-date, and free from malicious code.

This is your defense against malware, corrupted files, and integrity failures. It's all about ensuring the information your systems rely on is correct and secure.

Examples include:

- Deploying antivirus and endpoint protection
- Applying patches regularly
- Monitoring for unauthorized changes

How the Families Work Together

Each family on its own addresses a critical area, but the real power comes when they're implemented together. For example:

- Access Control relies on proper Identification and Authentication.
- Configuration Management supports System and Information Integrity.
- Risk Assessments guide how you implement Physical Protection or Audit Logging.

The point is: these aren't siloed requirements. They're meant to interlock and reinforce each other.

That's why approaching NIST 800-171 as a framework—not just a checklist—is so important. The controls work best when treated as part of a living, breathing security program.

Where to Begin

If this list feels overwhelming, that's okay. It's not meant to be a to-do list you complete in a day.

Many organizations start by focusing on:

- Access Control (Who can get in?)

- Identification and Authentication (How do we verify them?)

- Audit Logging (How do we know what's happening?)

- System Integrity (Are our systems patched and protected?)

These are foundational areas that support the rest. Later chapters in this book will walk through each control family in detail, showing you:

- What each requirement means

- Why it matters

- How to implement it using tools you already have (like Microsoft 365, Intune, or Entra)

- Tips for documenting your work and preparing for audits

Summary: Your NIST 800-171 Blueprint

The 14 control families in NIST 800-171 aren't just security buzzwords. They represent a practical, structured approach to protecting sensitive government data on non-federal systems.

As we move into the next chapters, we'll dive into each family in detail. You'll gain clarity on what each requirement asks for, and you'll learn how to implement those protections in the real world—without needing a PhD in cybersecurity.

This is your foundation. Take a moment to get comfortable with the names and general ideas here, and then get ready to roll up your sleeves.

Next up

We begin our deep-dive into the first control family—Access Control. You'll learn how to limit access to CUI, control user permissions, and enforce strong security practices from the very start.

Let's get to work.

Control Family: Access Control

Overview

Access Control is where it all begins.

In the world of cybersecurity, it's not just about whether your data is secure—it's about *who* can get to it, *when, how,* and *why.* Access control is the gatekeeper that determines who has permission to do what inside your systems.

In NIST 800-171, the Access Control family includes 22 specific requirements, making it one of the largest families in the entire framework. That's no accident. If you don't get access right, every other layer of protection becomes a lot less effective.

This family focuses on ensuring that:

- Only authorized users have access to CUI
- Access is granted based on roles and responsibilities
- Access is limited to only what is needed to perform a task
- Access can be reviewed, revoked, and tracked

In practical terms, access control isn't just about setting passwords. It's about managing who gets into the building, who gets into the systems, and what doors they can open once inside.

Why It Matters

Let's put it simply: if anyone can access everything, nothing is truly protected.

You can have world-class encryption, 24/7 monitoring, and automated threat detection—but if someone has too much access, or if an attacker steals valid credentials, they can bypass all of it.

That's why Access Control is often seen as your **first** and most important defense. It defines the boundaries of trust within your environment. It helps prevent:

- Data leaks from over-permissioned users
- Accidental misuse of sensitive information
- Lateral movement by attackers who breach one account
- Unauthorized sharing of CUI across systems or users

Access Control also sets the stage for compliance. Many government contracts, CMMC assessments, and industry regulations expect strict access enforcement. If your access controls are weak, your entire cybersecurity program can unravel.

Common Challenges

Despite its importance, access control is easier said than done. Here are some of the most common issues organizations face:

1. Over-Permissioned Users

It's common to give employees more access than they need—"just in case." Unfortunately, this increases risk. For example, if a user in accounting has access to engineering files, one phishing email could expose your entire operation.

2. Stale or Orphaned Accounts

Users leave organizations, change roles, or no longer need access to certain systems. Without a clear process to regularly review and remove access, these accounts linger—and they can be exploited.

3. Shared Accounts

Shared logins make it impossible to track individual accountability. You can't know who did what if three people are using the same credentials.

4. Unclear Roles and Responsibilities

If job roles aren't well-defined, assigning access becomes inconsistent. This makes it difficult to enforce least privilege or justify permissions during an audit.

5. Access Creep

Over time, users collect access to more systems or folders than they need—especially after switching departments or working on temporary projects. This often goes unnoticed unless regular access reviews are performed.

Example Implementation Steps

Let's break this into a practical plan. These steps can help you implement solid access controls across your organization.

Step 1: Define Roles and Responsibilities

Start by documenting user roles within your organization. What does a project manager need access to? What about a developer, a help desk technician, or a finance specialist?

Use the principle of least privilege—give users the *minimum access necessary* to do their jobs.

Step 2: Implement Role-Based Access Control (RBAC)

Once roles are defined, use them to structure your permission model. Group users based on their job function and assign permissions to the group—not the individual.

This simplifies user onboarding, reduces errors, and makes access reviews easier.

Step 3: Require Unique User Accounts

Every user should have a unique login. No shared accounts. This enables individual accountability and makes your audit trail far more reliable.

Step 4: Use Multi-Factor Authentication (MFA)

MFA adds a crucial layer of protection. Even if a password is compromised, a second form of verification (like a phone prompt or hardware key) helps stop unauthorized access.

Make MFA mandatory for:

- All users accessing CUI
- All administrative accounts
- Remote logins

Step 5: Limit Access to CUI Repositories

Identify where CUI is stored—file shares, databases, cloud storage, email—and lock them down. Only users with a legitimate business need should have access.

Where possible, segment networks or create separate document libraries specifically for CUI, and monitor access closely.

Step 6: Set Automatic Session Timeouts

For workstations and applications, configure automatic logouts after a period of inactivity. This prevents unauthorized access if someone forgets to lock their screen.

Step 7: Perform Regular Access Reviews

Set a schedule to review user access—quarterly is a good starting point. Involve department heads or supervisors to confirm users still need the permissions they have.

Be ready to document:

- Who has access
- What they have access to
- Why they need it
- When it was last reviewed

Step 8: Revoke Access Promptly

Have a clear offboarding process to immediately revoke access when employees leave or change roles. Automate this if possible with HR integration.

Microsoft / Intune / Azure / Entra M365 Alignment

Microsoft offers a powerful suite of tools that can help implement and enforce access control policies in line with NIST 800-171. Here's how:

Entra ID (formerly Azure AD)

- **RBAC**: Use Entra ID security groups to manage role-based permissions across services.
- **Conditional Access Policies**: Enforce rules based on user, device, location, and risk level (e.g., block access from untrusted countries).

- **MFA Enforcement**: Use Conditional Access to require MFA for all users or only high-risk scenarios.

Microsoft Intune

- **Compliance Policies**: Ensure that only compliant devices can access resources.

- **App Protection Policies**: Apply data access rules to mobile devices, even if they are personal (BYOD).

- **Endpoint Privilege Management**: Allow just-in-time elevation of local permissions for tasks that require admin rights—without giving permanent access.

Microsoft 365 and SharePoint

- **SharePoint Permissions**: Limit access to document libraries with fine-grained control.

- **Sensitivity Labels**: Tag CUI documents and enforce access based on classification.

- **Information Barriers**: Prevent specific groups from communicating or sharing files (useful for regulated environments or NDAs).

Microsoft Defender for Identity

- Detects suspicious access behavior, such as:
  - Impossible travel logins
  - Lateral movement by attackers
  - Unusual file access or privilege escalation

This monitoring supports both Audit and Access Control families by adding real-time insights.

Summary

Access Control is more than just passwords and permissions—it's a core part of your security posture and a critical component of NIST 800-171 compliance.

By implementing structured, role-based access policies and enforcing best practices like MFA, session timeouts, and access reviews, you dramatically reduce the chances of unauthorized access to CUI.

And by leveraging Microsoft 365, Entra, and Intune, you can automate and streamline much of this work—bringing your organization closer to both compliance and true security maturity.

Up Next

In the next chapter, we'll explore the Awareness and Training control family. You'll learn how to build a culture of security awareness, make training meaningful (not just a checkbox), and ensure your team is prepared to recognize and respond to threats—before they become incidents.

Let's keep going.

Control Family: Awareness and Training

Overview

Cybersecurity often starts with technology, but it succeeds or fails because of people.

You can have the strongest firewalls, the most advanced encryption, and the most locked-down access controls in the world—but if someone clicks on a phishing link or reuses a weak password across systems, all of that can come undone in an instant.

That's why the Awareness and Training control family in NIST 800-171 exists. It focuses on making sure that everyone in your organization—regardless of job title—understands their role in protecting Controlled Unclassified Information (CUI).

This family only contains three specific requirements, but don't let that fool you. The impact of getting it right—or wrong—can ripple across every area of your security program.

Awareness and Training isn't just about checking a box that says "completed training." It's about building a security-conscious culture that helps prevent threats before they happen and supports quick, smart responses when they do.

Why It Matters

People are your biggest asset—and your biggest vulnerability.

Attackers know that getting past your firewall might take hours or days of effort. But sending a well-crafted email that looks like it's from a government agency? That takes minutes, and unfortunately, someone might fall for it.

Security awareness is your human firewall. It gives your employees the instincts to recognize red flags, report suspicious activity, and avoid risky behavior that could expose CUI.

Here are just a few ways a lack of training can cause serious damage:

- An employee reuses their work password on a personal site that gets breached, exposing their government systems login

- Someone plugs an unapproved USB stick into a work machine, accidentally introducing malware

- A contractor shares a document containing CUI through an unencrypted personal email

- A well-meaning employee tries to "help" by downloading a cloud-based tool to speed up work, unintentionally creating a shadow IT risk

None of these mistakes come from bad intentions. They come from not knowing better.

That's why awareness and training matter. When your people understand what's at stake and how to act securely, your entire environment becomes safer.

Common Challenges

Many organizations struggle with security awareness—not because they don't want to do it, but because they treat it as a one-time event instead of a continuous process.

Here are some of the most common pitfalls:

1. Training Is Too Generic

Off-the-shelf training modules might satisfy a requirement on paper, but if they don't reflect your actual environment—your tools, your workflows, your threats—people tune out. Relevance matters.

2. No Role-Specific Training

An IT administrator and a front-desk receptionist face very different threats. Giving them the exact same training often leaves one confused and the other bored. Tailoring content by role improves engagement and effectiveness.

3. Lack of Reinforcement

Even great training fades from memory without reinforcement. If cybersecurity is only mentioned once a year during onboarding, it's unlikely to stick.

4. No Measurement or Tracking

If you're not tracking who completed training, how well they understood it, or whether behaviors changed afterward, you're missing key feedback to improve.

5. Awareness Becomes a Checklist

Security awareness should be an ongoing conversation. When it turns into a yearly checkbox, it loses its impact. Employees rush through it, forget it, and move on—leaving you no more secure than before.

Example Implementation Steps

Here's how you can build a meaningful Awareness and Training program that meets NIST 800-171 expectations and actually makes your organization more secure.

Step 1: Define Training Requirements for Each Role

Start by identifying what different people in your organization need to know. Your list might include:

- General staff
- Department managers
- IT administrators
- HR and legal teams
- Executives
- Third-party vendors or contractors

From there, identify what specific CUI-related risks they're exposed to and build content around those risks. This ensures that everyone receives training that's relevant to their job.

Step 2: Develop or Acquire Engaging Content

Your training program should go beyond reading documents. Consider using:

- Short videos and real-world examples
- Interactive quizzes
- Phishing simulations
- Internal stories of past incidents (anonymized, if needed)

If you're using a third-party vendor, choose one that allows customization and integrates with your identity or HR system for automated tracking.

Step 3: Set a Recurring Training Schedule

Awareness isn't one-and-done. Training should be:

- Delivered during onboarding for all new employees

- Repeated at least annually
- Updated regularly to reflect new threats, tools, and business changes

Many organizations also run monthly or quarterly "micro-training" topics, such as a short video or article on a trending threat or a new company policy.

Step 4: Launch a Phishing Simulation Program

Phishing remains the number one cause of breaches. Simulated phishing campaigns:

- Test real-world behavior
- Identify users who may need extra support
- Normalize the idea that suspicious emails should be reported

Make sure these campaigns are educational, not punitive. The goal is to teach, not shame.

Step 5: Create a Clear Reporting Path

When employees see something suspicious, they need to know what to do. Make sure they can easily report:

- Phishing emails
- Unauthorized system access
- Unusual system behavior
- Security concerns

Whether it's a dedicated email address, a Teams channel, or a help desk ticket form, make the process easy and stress-free.

Step 6: Track Participation and Completion

Use your LMS (Learning Management System) or another training platform to track who has completed required training. Document attendance and completion logs to satisfy auditors or regulatory reviews.

You can also issue certificates or badges internally to acknowledge participation and promote a culture of accountability.

Step 7: Reinforce with Culture

The most effective security awareness programs are the ones people actually talk about. Find ways to bring security into the daily rhythm of your organization, such as:

- Security tip of the week in team meetings
- Posters or digital signage in shared spaces
- Gamified challenges or internal contests
- Newsletters highlighting common threats and employee wins

When people see security as part of their job—not just IT's job—your whole organization benefits.

Microsoft / Intune / Azure / Entra M365 Alignment

Microsoft tools can support and enhance your Awareness and Training efforts in several practical ways.

Microsoft 365 Compliance Center

- Use Communication Compliance to monitor risky behavior, such as inappropriate sharing of CUI or policy violations in Teams, email, and SharePoint

- Set Information Governance policies to highlight improper handling of labeled documents and use those findings in training scenarios

Microsoft Defender for Office 365

- Launch attack simulations that send fake phishing messages to employees and track who clicks

- Customize simulation difficulty by department or job role

- Integrate simulation results with training platforms to offer tailored follow-up

Intune and Endpoint Manager

- Push required training links or files to user desktops and mobile devices

- Use device compliance policies to require training completion before granting access to sensitive resources

- Send alerts or reminders through Microsoft Teams or Endpoint notifications

Entra ID (Azure Active Directory)

- Use dynamic security groups to automatically enroll users into different training paths based on department, role, or region

- Integrate with single sign-on to streamline access to training systems and log user completion

Viva Learning and Microsoft Teams

- Assign, promote, and track training directly within the Teams interface

- Use Viva Learning to surface security content from Microsoft Learn, LinkedIn Learning, or custom content

- Schedule reminders and monitor participation as part of everyday collaboration

Summary

Awareness and Training isn't just a compliance requirement—it's a foundation for a secure workplace.

By helping people understand their role in protecting CUI and giving them the tools to respond to real-world threats, you create a culture where security is everyone's responsibility. That culture, reinforced by ongoing training and leadership support, can prevent the most common (and costly) types of breaches.

With just three core requirements, this control family may be small—but when implemented well, its impact can be enormous.

Coming Up Next

Next, we'll dive into Audit and Accountability—a control family that focuses on how to record system activity, track user actions, and review logs to detect suspicious behavior. We'll explore how to make auditing useful, not overwhelming, and how to use tools you already have to build an effective logging and accountability strategy.

Let's keep building.

Control Family: Audit and Accountability

Overview

In cybersecurity, seeing what's happening inside your systems is just as important as locking them down.

The Audit and Accountability family in NIST 800-171 ensures that organizations don't operate in the dark. It focuses on logging, monitoring, and reviewing system activity so that you can detect unauthorized actions, investigate incidents, and hold people accountable for what happens in your environment.

This control family contains nine requirements, all centered around creating, protecting, reviewing, and responding to audit logs.

If you think of your security system like a building, access control might be the locks on the doors—but audit logs are your security cameras, recording who entered, when, and what they did. Without these records, you'd have no idea if someone was walking the halls when they shouldn't be.

Why It Matters

Modern cyberattacks don't happen all at once—they unfold over time. A breached account might be used quietly for days or even weeks before an attacker takes action. The only way to catch this kind of activity early—or to understand what happened after a breach—is through detailed audit logs.

Audit and accountability serves three critical functions:

1. **Detecting malicious or suspicious behavior**
   Logs give you visibility into things like failed login attempts, privilege escalations, or unusual data access patterns—early warning signs of compromise.

2. **Reconstructing events after an incident**
   If a breach does happen, logs are often the only way to figure out what went wrong, how far the attacker got, and what needs to be fixed.

3. **Establishing accountability**
   Logs tie actions to individuals, helping ensure that users are held responsible for what happens under their credentials. This supports both internal policy enforcement and external audit readiness.

Audit logs are also a key requirement for compliance. Most regulators, including those involved in CMMC, expect logs to be generated, protected, and regularly reviewed. Without a functioning logging system, it's nearly impossible to prove your controls are working.

Common Challenges

Implementing a strong audit program often runs into the same set of obstacles:

1. Logging Isn't Centralized

When logs are spread across multiple systems—firewalls, workstations, file servers, email platforms—it's difficult to collect them, correlate events, or get a complete picture of what's happening.

2. Logging Isn't Enabled

Many organizations assume logging is turned on by default. Often, it isn't. If audit settings aren't configured on endpoints, cloud services, and servers, you'll miss key data.

3. Logs Are Incomplete or Overwhelming

It's possible to collect too little—or too much. Logs that are missing key details (like user IDs or timestamps) are useless. Logs that flood your team with irrelevant data become noise.

4. Nobody Reviews the Logs

Collecting logs is just step one. If no one is reviewing them—or if the review process isn't consistent—you may not catch problems until it's too late.

5. Poor Retention or Protection

If logs are overwritten after a few days or stored in locations that can be edited or deleted by unauthorized users, their integrity is compromised.

Example Implementation Steps

Let's walk through a practical approach to implementing Audit and Accountability controls that meet both NIST 800-171 and real-world needs.

Step 1: Identify What Needs to Be Logged

Start by identifying critical systems and data sources, including:

- Domain controllers and authentication services
- File servers storing CUI
- End-user workstations
- Firewalls, VPNs, and network appliances
- Cloud services like Microsoft 365 and SharePoint
- Administrative tools (e.g., PowerShell, remote access software)

For each, define what events should be logged. Key examples include:

- Successful and failed login attempts

- File creation, modification, or deletion

- Privilege escalations

- Changes to access permissions

- System configuration changes

Step 2: Enable Logging Across All Endpoints

Make sure logging is turned on and configured correctly. On Windows systems, this typically involves enabling audit policies via Group Policy or Intune. For cloud platforms, it may involve enabling mailbox auditing or API logging features.

Ensure that logs include:

- Username

- Timestamp

- IP address or host machine

- Action taken (e.g., login, file access)

- Success or failure of the action

Step 3: Centralize Log Collection

Use a Security Information and Event Management (SIEM) system or logging aggregator to pull logs into a central location. This makes correlation, analysis, and alerting much easier.

Common SIEM tools include:

- Microsoft Sentinel

- Splunk

- LogRhythm

- Elastic Stack

If a full SIEM is out of scope, even a centralized file share or log-forwarding agent can help get started.

Step 4: Protect the Logs

Logs should be:

- Write-once (users shouldn't be able to alter or delete them)
- Backed up regularly
- Access-controlled to prevent unauthorized viewing or tampering

Audit trail integrity is essential. If attackers can cover their tracks by editing or deleting logs, the entire system loses value.

Step 5: Set a Review Schedule

Assign responsibility for reviewing logs—ideally daily or weekly, depending on your risk level. Use automated alerts to flag:

- Unusual login times
- Repeated failed logins
- Admin activity outside of normal hours
- Sudden changes to large numbers of files or settings

This doesn't need to be a manual grind. Start small and focus on patterns or indicators of compromise.

Step 6: Retain Logs for an Appropriate Period

Set a log retention policy based on your contractual or legal obligations. NIST doesn't mandate a specific time frame, but at least 90 days of active review data and 6–12 months of archival storage is a good baseline.

Step 7: Document Your Process

Auditors will want to see that you're not just collecting logs, but actually reviewing and acting on them.

Keep records that show:

- What logs are collected
- Where they're stored
- Who reviews them
- What alerts or reports are generated
- Any corrective actions taken based on findings

Microsoft / Intune / Azure / Entra M365 Alignment

Microsoft offers powerful tools for implementing Audit and Accountability requirements effectively across both on-prem and cloud environments.

Microsoft 365 Compliance Center

- **Audit Search**: Use built-in audit logs to track user and admin actions across Exchange, SharePoint, OneDrive, and Teams.
- **Advanced Audit (with E5 licensing)**: Provides longer retention and deeper audit events, such as mailbox reads or data access from outside the organization.

Microsoft Defender for Endpoint

- Provides behavioral monitoring and device-level logs
- Detects lateral movement, privilege escalation, and file modifications

- Integrates with Microsoft Sentinel for deeper analysis

Microsoft Sentinel (SIEM)
- Aggregates logs from Microsoft and third-party sources
- Correlates activity across systems to detect complex threats
- Supports automated playbooks for incident response

Intune and Endpoint Manager
- Enforces audit policy settings via configuration profiles
- Tracks device compliance status and user activity
- Logs configuration changes, policy assignments, and compliance results

Entra ID (Azure Active Directory)
- Provides sign-in logs and audit logs for identity-related activity
- Tracks conditional access events, risky sign-ins, and admin actions
- Integrates with Microsoft 365 for unified alerting

Summary

Audit and Accountability may not be the most glamorous part of cybersecurity, but it's one of the most vital. Without logging, you're blind to what's happening in your systems. Without review, you're vulnerable to threats that slip past the perimeter.

Implementing strong audit practices not only helps you detect attacks and investigate incidents—it also builds trust, transparency, and resilience across your organization.

Start by logging the basics. Centralize your records. Set review processes that your team can actually follow. Over time, you'll build a living system that supports both compliance and security maturity.

Coming Up Next

Next, we'll explore Configuration Management, the control family that helps you lock down system settings, prevent unauthorized changes, and maintain consistency across your IT environment. You'll learn how to avoid configuration drift and use tools like Intune to enforce secure baselines with confidence.

Let's keep going.

Control Family: Configuration Management

Overview

Every device, server, application, and network component in your environment has settings that determine how it behaves. Some of these settings control basic functionality, while others govern how secure—or vulnerable—your system really is.

The Configuration Management control family in NIST 800-171 focuses on establishing, enforcing, and monitoring secure configurations across your organization's systems. It ensures that your systems aren't left with default settings, unneeded features, or unpredictable behaviors that could introduce security risks.

This family contains nine requirements, each designed to help you create a consistent, hardened environment where CUI can be protected reliably.

At its core, configuration management is about answering two critical questions:

- Do we know how our systems are supposed to be configured?
- Can we prove they're still configured that way today?

Why It Matters

Most successful cyberattacks don't start with hackers breaking through some high-tech barrier. They start with a misconfigured system—an open port, a default password, an unpatched application, or an exposed service that no one realized was running.

Configuration issues open the door to all kinds of threats:

- Unauthorized access

- Privilege escalation
- Malware exploitation
- Data leakage

And because today's environments are dynamic—with frequent updates, new device enrollments, and cloud-based services—it's easy for systems to drift from their intended state. A single configuration change can introduce a critical weakness.

Configuration management prevents this by enforcing standardized, secure settings across your systems, and by keeping a record of all changes so you can quickly detect and respond to anything unexpected.

Common Challenges

Organizations often underestimate how hard it is to manage system configurations effectively. Here are some of the challenges that come up most often:

1. Lack of Baseline Standards

Without a clearly defined "golden image" or baseline configuration, teams often set up systems on the fly—leading to inconsistent security across devices or environments.

2. Manual Configuration

When settings are applied manually, it's easy to forget steps, skip patches, or apply inconsistent controls. This also makes systems harder to audit or replicate later.

3. Configuration Drift

Even with a solid starting point, systems tend to drift over time as updates are applied, users change settings, or administrators troubleshoot problems. Over time, those small changes accumulate into major risk.

4. Unnecessary Features and Services

Many systems come with features enabled by default that aren't needed for your organization. These unused services can become attack vectors if not disabled.

5. Poor Documentation and Change Control

Without a process to review, approve, and document configuration changes, organizations often lose visibility into what changed and why—a serious problem during incident investigations or audits.

Example Implementation Steps

A strong configuration management process doesn't have to be complicated—but it does need to be consistent. Here's a step-by-step approach to implementing this control family in your environment.

Step 1: Define Secure Baseline Configurations

Start by identifying which systems handle or interact with CUI. These typically include:

- Laptops and desktops
- Servers (on-prem or cloud)
- Network devices
- Mobile phones and tablets
- Cloud applications (e.g., Microsoft 365, Azure AD)

For each system type, define a secure baseline configuration. This might include:

- Enforced screen lock and timeout settings
- Disabled local admin accounts
- Blocked unused ports or services
- Encrypted storage

- Disabled macros in Office files
- Minimum versions of installed software

Your baseline should reflect:

- Industry best practices (such as CIS Benchmarks or Microsoft's security baselines)
- Compliance needs specific to CUI protection

Document these baselines clearly so that administrators can reference and apply them during deployments.

Step 2: Apply Configurations Consistently

Use automation wherever possible to apply your baselines across systems. Manual configurations not only increase the chance for error—they also make the process slower and harder to scale.

Tools like Intune, Group Policy, and configuration scripts can help:

- Push standard settings to new and existing devices
- Prevent users from altering enforced settings
- Reapply settings if a user or update changes them

Step 3: Disable Unnecessary Services and Features

Every service running on a system is a potential attack vector. Go through your device and server configurations and turn off anything not essential to business operations.

Examples include:

- File sharing services on end-user laptops
- Remote desktop protocol (RDP) on non-admin systems
- Bluetooth or Wi-Fi on stationary devices
- Built-in guest accounts or legacy protocols

This minimizes your attack surface and makes your environment easier to monitor.

Step 4: Monitor for Configuration Changes

Once your configurations are in place, you'll need to monitor them to ensure nothing drifts out of compliance.

Use monitoring tools to:

- Track registry changes or setting modifications
- Alert on unauthorized software installation
- Compare current configurations against your baseline

This allows you to detect unexpected or risky changes early—whether they're the result of human error, malware, or insider threats.

Step 5: Establish a Change Control Process

Not all changes are bad—sometimes systems need to be updated or adjusted. But changes should always go through a formal process.

Your change control policy should include:

- A way to request changes
- An approval and testing process
- Documentation of what changed and why
- A rollback plan in case something goes wrong

This ensures that changes are made intentionally and with accountability.

Step 6: Conduct Periodic Configuration Reviews

Set a schedule (e.g., quarterly or bi-annually) to formally review system configurations and compare them against your defined baselines. Use this time to:

- Check for configuration drift
- Reassess baseline settings based on new threats or business needs
- Validate that automation tools are working as expected

Microsoft / Intune / Azure / Entra M365 Alignment

Microsoft provides several tools to help implement configuration management in a scalable and policy-driven way, especially in cloud-connected environments.

Microsoft Intune

- **Configuration Profiles**: Apply security and device settings (such as BitLocker, password policies, screen lock, and app restrictions) across Windows, macOS, iOS, and Android.

- **Endpoint Security Policies**: Apply hardening rules based on Microsoft-recommended baselines.

- **Custom Scripts**: Deploy PowerShell or shell scripts to enforce or validate configuration settings.

- **Compliance Policies**: Flag devices that fall out of baseline or fail to meet required conditions.

Group Policy (via Active Directory or Intune)

- For environments still using traditional Active Directory, Group Policy remains a powerful tool to manage settings like:
  - Windows Defender configuration
  - USB port access
  - System service startup rules

Group Policy can also be layered with cloud policies using Intune co-management or MDM GPOs.

Microsoft Security Baselines

- Microsoft publishes security configuration baselines for Windows, Microsoft Edge, and Microsoft 365. These are pre-tested collections of security settings aligned with best practices.

- You can import these baselines into Intune and apply them to your devices as a starting point, adjusting where needed.

Azure Policy

- For Azure-based virtual machines or services, use Azure Policy to enforce configurations such as:

  o Resource tagging

  o Encryption at rest

  o Approved VM types

  o Deployment in approved regions

This brings configuration management to your cloud workloads and supports compliance tracking.

Microsoft Defender for Endpoint

- Monitors system configurations and alerts you when changes deviate from expected norms.

- Detects and logs when critical services are modified, disabled, or reconfigured.

Summary

Configuration Management might sound like a background process—but it plays a frontline role in keeping your systems secure and compliant.

By defining and enforcing consistent, secure settings across your environment, you reduce the risk of vulnerabilities, prevent misconfigurations, and give yourself a solid foundation for responding to threats and audits alike.

A strong configuration strategy doesn't just protect CUI—it brings predictability, efficiency, and peace of mind to your entire IT operation.

Coming Up Next

In the next chapter, we'll tackle Identification and Authentication—the family that defines how users and devices prove who they are before gaining access to systems and data. We'll break down how to implement secure login practices, reduce identity-related risks, and apply multi-factor authentication across your Microsoft ecosystem.

Let's keep going.

Control Family: Identification and Authentication

Overview

At the foundation of every secure system lies a simple but powerful idea: prove who you are before you get access.

That's the core of the Identification and Authentication control family in NIST 800-171. It focuses on how users, devices, and systems verify their identity before being allowed to connect to anything that stores or processes Controlled Unclassified Information (CUI).

This family contains eleven requirements, and each one is about ensuring that:

- Every user is uniquely identified

- Authentication is strong enough to prevent impersonation

- Unauthorized devices and users can't slip through the cracks

Whether it's a human logging into a laptop, a script calling an API, or a device joining a network, the question is always the same: "Can we trust that this is who they say they are?"

And in today's threat landscape, trust must be earned—not assumed.

Why It Matters

Think about how most cyberattacks begin. The attacker doesn't usually start by cracking an encrypted database or exploiting a firewall. More often than not, they start by stealing or guessing credentials.

A leaked password. A reused login. A poorly secured administrator account.

If you can prevent unauthorized access through strong identity verification, you block a huge portion of potential threats before they even start.

Identification and Authentication is critical because:

- **Stolen credentials are common**: Phishing, password reuse, and data breaches all feed the underground economy of usernames and passwords.

- **Privileged access is highly targeted**: If an attacker gets into an admin account, they can bypass nearly every other control.

- **Remote work increases risk**: With employees logging in from home, hotels, or mobile devices, identity becomes the new perimeter.

Strong identity controls aren't just a best practice—they're a frontline defense.

Common Challenges

Even though identity and authentication seem straightforward, many organizations struggle to implement them securely and consistently. Here's why:

1. Weak or Reused Passwords

Users often reuse passwords across multiple accounts, choose simple ones, or fall for phishing attacks that expose them. Without enforcement and training, these habits can quickly lead to compromise.

2. Shared Accounts

Accounts that are used by multiple people—such as "admin" or "helpdesk"—destroy traceability. If something goes wrong, you can't tie it back to a specific person.

3. Inconsistent Authentication Policies

Some systems might require MFA, while others only ask for a password. When policies vary across platforms, users look for shortcuts—and attackers look for the weakest link.

4. Unmanaged Devices and Legacy Systems

Devices that aren't enrolled in your management tools may bypass authentication requirements altogether. Legacy systems might not support modern protocols or MFA, leaving gaps in protection.

5. Lack of Audit Trails

Without logs showing who authenticated and when, you can't spot anomalies or respond to incidents effectively.

Example Implementation Steps

Let's walk through how to implement secure identification and authentication practices that align with NIST 800-171—and support your broader security strategy.

Step 1: Assign Unique User IDs

Every user should have a unique login. Avoid shared accounts at all costs. Even for temporary access, issue unique credentials and disable them after use.

If you must use service accounts (for scripts or automation), make sure:

- They're not tied to individual users
- Their use is well-documented
- They have the least privilege required
- They're monitored like any other account

Step 2: Enforce Strong Password Policies

Implement password policies that:

- Require complexity (uppercase, lowercase, numbers, symbols)
- Prevent reuse of recent passwords
- Enforce expiration after a reasonable time (e.g., 90 days)
- Block passwords from known breach lists

Avoid making password rules so complicated that users write them down or use predictable patterns—strike a balance between strength and usability.

Step 3: Implement Multi-Factor Authentication (MFA)

MFA is one of the most effective ways to protect user identities. Require MFA for:

- All users accessing CUI
- All administrative accounts
- All remote logins

MFA can include:

- Authenticator apps (Microsoft Authenticator, DUO, etc.)
- Hardware tokens or smartcards
- Biometric logins
- Phone-based OTPs (used with caution)

Avoid relying on SMS alone, as it can be vulnerable to SIM-swapping and interception.

Step 4: Secure System-to-System Authentication

APIs, scripts, and automation often authenticate using tokens or certificates. Apply strong practices here too:

- Use short-lived authentication tokens
- Rotate secrets regularly
- Limit scope and permissions of service accounts

Ensure that automated processes don't rely on stored plaintext passwords or hard-coded credentials in scripts.

Step 5: Restrict and Monitor Admin Accounts

Admin accounts should:

- Be used only when needed (just-in-time access is ideal)
- Be separate from regular user accounts
- Require MFA and session logging
- Be limited in number and scope

Consider using privileged access management (PAM) tools to further control and audit usage.

Step 6: Implement Account Lockouts and Timeouts

To reduce brute force attacks:

- Lock accounts after a set number of failed login attempts
- Require password resets through secure channels
- Automatically sign out users after a period of inactivity

This helps protect accounts from unauthorized guessing or unattended sessions.

Step 7: Log and Review Authentication Events

Track all login activity—successful and failed—for both users and systems. Monitor for:

- Repeated failures
- Logins from unusual locations or times
- Unexpected access to sensitive systems

Correlate login events with other system activity to catch signs of compromise.

Step 8: Deactivate Accounts Promptly

Have a defined process to:

- Disable accounts immediately when users leave the organization
- Remove permissions when roles change
- Periodically review inactive accounts for cleanup

This prevents forgotten or unused accounts from becoming backdoors.

Microsoft / Intune / Azure / Entra M365 Alignment

Microsoft's identity and security ecosystem offers robust tools for implementing Identification and Authentication controls across both cloud and on-prem environments.

Entra ID (Azure Active Directory)

- **MFA**: Enforce MFA through Conditional Access policies across all users and apps.

- **Password Protection**: Block weak or leaked passwords using Entra ID's banned password list.

- **Identity Protection**: Detect risky sign-ins and user behavior with built-in machine learning models.

- **Single Sign-On (SSO)**: Reduce password sprawl by enabling secure SSO across SaaS and on-prem apps.

Microsoft Intune

- **Device Compliance Policies**: Require that devices meet security standards before allowing sign-in.

- **User Credential Policies**: Push configurations that enforce lock screens, password lengths, and authentication requirements.

- **Managed Device Enrollment**: Ensure that only known, enrolled devices can access sensitive resources.

Microsoft Defender for Identity

- Monitors user behavior across your domain and detects suspicious sign-in activity.

- Alerts you to lateral movement, brute-force attacks, and credential theft.

- Helps correlate identity events with endpoint and network telemetry.

Microsoft 365 Admin Center

- **Audit Logs**: Track sign-in activity across Exchange, SharePoint, Teams, and more.

- **Security Reports**: Identify users not enrolled in MFA or using legacy authentication.

- **Alert Policies**: Trigger alerts when suspicious sign-ins or credential usage occurs.

Windows Hello for Business

- Enables secure, passwordless sign-in using biometrics or PINs tied to the user's hardware.

- Helps reduce password-based risks while maintaining strong authentication.

Summary

Identification and Authentication may sound simple, but it's one of the most powerful tools in your security arsenal. It's also one of the most targeted.

By requiring unique identities, enforcing strong authentication, and removing outdated or insecure methods, you significantly reduce the chances of unauthorized access to CUI.

With Microsoft tools like Entra ID, Intune, and Defender, you can centralize and streamline your identity controls—making them not only stronger, but easier to manage and scale.

Coming Up Next

In the next chapter, we'll explore Incident Response—a crucial control family that helps you prepare for and respond to security events. We'll cover how to build an incident response plan, assign roles, test your readiness, and recover quickly when things go wrong.

Security incidents aren't a matter of "if"—they're a matter of "when." Let's get ready.

Control Family: Incident Response

Overview

No matter how strong your defenses are, security incidents will happen.

Whether it's a phishing attack, unauthorized access, data leakage, or suspicious user behavior, the reality is that no system is invincible. The difference between an inconvenience and a disaster often comes down to how well you respond when something goes wrong.

The Incident Response control family in NIST 800-171 focuses on making sure your organization is prepared to detect, respond to, contain, and recover from security incidents.

This control family includes three key requirements:

1. Creating and implementing an incident response plan

2. Tracking, documenting, and reporting incidents

3. Testing and refining the response process

It's not about eliminating every threat—it's about being ready when one appears.

Why It Matters

When a security incident happens, time is everything.

The faster your team can detect it, confirm what's happening, and take action, the less damage it's likely to cause. And if your team doesn't know what to do—or doesn't realize something is happening—an incident can escalate quickly and quietly.

An effective incident response program helps you:

- Minimize downtime and data loss

- Contain threats before they spread

- Preserve evidence for investigation

- Demonstrate compliance and accountability

- Recover operations faster and more confidently

For organizations handling Controlled Unclassified Information (CUI), the stakes are even higher. Incident response isn't just about protecting your systems—it's about safeguarding information entrusted to you by the U.S. government.

Common Challenges

Incident response isn't just about reacting. It's about planning and practicing—two things many organizations neglect until it's too late.

Here are common challenges that weaken incident response:

1. No Written Plan

Many organizations have an idea of what they *might* do during an incident, but without a formal, documented plan, response efforts are inconsistent and error-prone.

2. Unclear Roles and Communication

When an incident occurs, who's in charge? Who contacts leadership? Who gathers logs? Without defined roles, teams waste precious time figuring out what to do while the incident escalates.

3. Infrequent Testing

Even a well-written plan can fall apart if it's never tested. Plans that look good on paper often fail under pressure because they haven't been practiced.

4. Poor Detection and Reporting

If staff don't know how to recognize and report incidents—or if detection tools are weak—response starts too late, and attackers gain more ground.

5. Lack of Coordination Across Tools

Your security tools might detect threats, but if they're not integrated or monitored effectively, you may miss critical alerts or struggle to investigate events efficiently.

Example Implementation Steps

A successful incident response process is like a fire drill—it should be clear, rehearsed, and instinctive. Here's how to build one.

Step 1: Write an Incident Response Plan

Start with a formal, documented plan that includes:

- Definition of a security incident
- Roles and responsibilities (incident manager, communications lead, technical responders)
- Communication strategy (internal and external)
- Escalation procedures
- Containment and remediation steps
- Reporting obligations (especially if CUI is involved)
- Post-incident review process

Keep it simple, actionable, and accessible—not a 100-page document no one will read.

Step 2: Establish an Incident Response Team

Form a team that can be activated during a security event. This doesn't have to be a full-time role for everyone, but responsibilities must be clear.

Typical roles include:

- **Incident Commander**: Oversees and coordinates response
- **Security Analysts**: Investigate and contain threats
- **Communications Lead**: Manages internal and external updates
- **IT Admins**: Execute containment and recovery tasks
- **Legal/Compliance**: Assesses regulatory impact and reporting requirements

Assign backups for each role, and make sure contact info is kept current.

Step 3: Define Incident Categories and Severity Levels

Not all incidents require the same response. Define categories such as:

- **Low**: Single phishing attempt, blocked malware
- **Medium**: Unauthorized access to non-sensitive systems
- **High**: CUI compromise, ransomware, persistent attacker activity

For each severity level, define what steps must be taken and who should be notified.

Step 4: Implement Detection and Monitoring Tools

You can't respond to what you don't see. Use tools that:

- Detect unusual logins, privilege escalation, or file access
- Alert on malware, lateral movement, or policy violations
- Log user and system activity for later investigation

Ensure that alerts are routed to the right people, and tune them to reduce false positives.

Step 5: Establish an Incident Reporting Mechanism

Make it easy for staff to report suspected incidents. Options include:

- A dedicated email address (e.g., security@yourcompany.com)
- A Microsoft Teams channel
- A helpdesk ticket category for security
- A "Report Phishing" button in Outlook

Train employees to report:

- Phishing emails
- Suspicious logins or system behavior
- Unexpected data loss or file corruption

Encourage reporting without fear of punishment—it's better to be alerted early.

Step 6: Conduct Regular Tabletop Exercises

Run simulated scenarios at least annually to practice your response plan. Include:

- A mock incident (e.g., a ransomware attack or stolen credentials)
- Role-played responses from team members
- Time-pressured decision making
- A post-mortem discussion to identify gaps

Use what you learn to update the plan and improve readiness.

Step 7: Document and Learn from Real Incidents

When real incidents occur:

- Document what happened, who was involved, and how it was resolved

- Identify root causes

- Highlight what went well and what didn't

- Update your IR plan and training accordingly

This continuous improvement loop is essential to maturing your security posture.

Microsoft / Intune / Azure / Entra M365 Alignment

Microsoft provides a rich ecosystem of tools to help detect, respond to, and manage security incidents effectively.

Microsoft Defender for Endpoint

- Detects threats such as malware, lateral movement, credential theft, and zero-day exploits

- Correlates alerts into incidents and guides response actions

- Provides forensic data for investigation (file history, process trees, network activity)

Microsoft Sentinel

- A cloud-native SIEM that aggregates logs and alerts from across your environment

- Creates incidents from correlated data

- Supports playbooks for automated response (e.g., disable a user, block an IP, notify the team)
- Enables advanced hunting through Kusto Query Language (KQL)

Microsoft 365 Defender

- Unifies threat data across email, endpoints, identities, and cloud apps
- Automatically groups related alerts into a single incident view
- Supports investigation, containment, and remediation workflows

Intune and Endpoint Manager

- Wipe or lock compromised devices remotely
- Push updated configuration policies or scripts during response
- Enforce conditional access to block affected users or devices during an incident

Entra ID (Azure Active Directory)

- Detects risky sign-ins and unfamiliar behavior
- Logs access attempts and user activity for investigation
- Supports Conditional Access to isolate high-risk accounts automatically

Microsoft Purview Compliance Portal

- Helps track incidents involving data loss or CUI exposure
- Supports insider risk management for early detection of risky behavior

- Documents incidents and investigations for audit and compliance purposes

Summary

Incident Response isn't just a cybersecurity practice—it's a business survival skill.

By preparing your people, defining your processes, and leveraging the right tools, you can turn a potentially chaotic crisis into a structured, calm, and effective response.

With a strong incident response plan in place, your organization won't just survive attacks—it will emerge stronger from them.

Coming Up Next

Next, we'll dive into Maintenance, the control family focused on securing how systems are serviced and maintained. You'll learn how to manage both remote and on-site maintenance activities without creating new risks or compliance gaps.

Let's keep building your secure foundation.

Control Family: Maintenance

Overview

Every system eventually needs maintenance. Whether it's applying patches, updating software, replacing hardware, or running diagnostics, maintenance is a normal and necessary part of managing IT systems.

But here's the catch: maintenance activities can introduce risk. If not handled properly, a routine task—like a firmware update or remote support session—can become the entry point for a breach.

The Maintenance control family in NIST 800-171 focuses on making sure that only authorized maintenance activities are performed, and that they are done securely, under controlled conditions, and with proper oversight.

There are six requirements in this family. Each one is designed to ensure that whether maintenance is scheduled, remote, or emergency-based, it doesn't compromise your ability to protect Controlled Unclassified Information (CUI).

Why It Matters

Maintenance might seem like a background task, but it often involves:

- Access to sensitive systems
- Administrative privileges
- Temporary bypassing of security settings
- External tools or technicians

If these activities are unmonitored, unapproved, or performed without proper safeguards, they can lead to serious problems.

Examples of maintenance-related risks include:

- A third-party vendor connecting to your network remotely without MFA

- A technician installing unapproved software that introduces vulnerabilities

- A system update unintentionally disabling security settings

- Unauthorized use of diagnostic tools that access CUI

Good maintenance practices reduce these risks by enforcing controls around who can perform maintenance, how it's done, and what happens afterward.

Common Challenges

Many organizations view maintenance as a routine IT task, not a security concern. This leads to several recurring issues:

1. Informal Maintenance Procedures

Without documented maintenance policies, staff may make ad-hoc decisions, skip approval steps, or forget to document changes.

2. Unmonitored Remote Access

Remote maintenance tools—like RDP, VPNs, or remote desktop software—are often left running or accessible to unauthorized users, increasing attack surface.

3. Third-Party Maintenance Without Vetting

Vendors or contractors may be allowed to perform maintenance without proper background checks, access controls, or logging.

4. Inadequate Tracking and Documentation

When maintenance isn't logged, you lose visibility into changes made to systems. This makes it difficult to troubleshoot problems or investigate incidents later.

5. Maintenance Causing Configuration Drift

Updates or patches can overwrite secure baselines or re-enable services that were intentionally disabled, introducing risk or compliance issues.

Example Implementation Steps

Implementing secure maintenance practices doesn't mean slowing things down. It means introducing the right level of control and oversight to ensure systems remain both functional and secure.

Step 1: Create a Maintenance Policy

Your policy should define:

- What types of maintenance require prior approval
- Who is authorized to perform maintenance (internal staff, contractors, vendors)
- Required documentation and change control steps
- How to handle emergency maintenance
- Logging and audit requirements

Make sure the policy is accessible, realistic, and enforced consistently.

Step 2: Define Authorized Maintenance Roles

Not everyone should have the ability to perform system maintenance. Clearly define which users or roles have permission to:

- Install updates or patches
- Reconfigure systems
- Access diagnostic tools
- Modify system files

Limit these permissions based on the principle of least privilege, and review them regularly.

Step 3: Require Supervision or Monitoring

For maintenance activities—especially those involving CUI systems—implement safeguards such as:

- Activity logging and session recording
- Requiring dual control or supervision
- Time-limited access for vendors or contractors

If someone is performing sensitive maintenance, their actions should be observable and traceable.

Step 4: Secure Remote Maintenance

Remote maintenance introduces additional risk, especially if it bypasses normal network protections. Enforce these safeguards:

- Require MFA for remote sessions
- Use secure, approved remote access tools (e.g., Intune Remote Help, Microsoft LAPS)
- Log and review all remote sessions
- Prohibit remote maintenance when systems contain highly sensitive CUI, unless explicitly authorized and protected

Disable remote access services (like RDP or third-party remote control software) when not in use.

Step 5: Vet and Manage External Maintenance Providers

If you rely on outside vendors for hardware, software, or system support:

- Conduct background checks and vetting as appropriate
- Include security requirements in contracts and service agreements
- Limit vendor access to only what's necessary
- Require them to follow your internal procedures and policies

All third-party maintenance should be scheduled, approved, and monitored.

Step 6: Track and Document All Maintenance

For every maintenance event, keep a log that includes:

- Date and time
- System(s) involved
- Purpose of maintenance
- Technician or vendor name
- Actions performed
- Any issues encountered
- Resulting system status (success, failure, follow-up needed)

This log helps with troubleshooting, compliance audits, and incident investigations.

Step 7: Revalidate System Security After Maintenance

Maintenance can sometimes undo security settings or change configurations unintentionally. After maintenance is completed:

- Run a system health and security check
- Verify that the system still meets your configuration baseline
- Apply any missing policies or patches

- Reassess system compliance with internal security controls

This step helps catch issues before they become vulnerabilities.

Microsoft / Intune / Azure / Entra M365 Alignment

Microsoft tools provide several capabilities for securely managing system maintenance—especially in remote and hybrid environments.

Microsoft Intune

- **Windows Update Policies**: Automate patching across devices while maintaining control over timing and approvals.

- **Endpoint Remediation Scripts**: Automatically verify or restore secure configurations after maintenance.

- **Intune Remote Help**: Secure remote support with session control, audit logging, and role-based access.

- **Device Compliance Monitoring**: Ensure post-maintenance devices remain compliant with your policies.

Microsoft Endpoint Manager

- Allows deployment of maintenance-related scripts and updates at scale

- Integrates with Configuration Manager for hybrid maintenance workflows

- Provides inventory and reporting of maintenance actions across the fleet

Microsoft Defender for Endpoint

- Tracks system changes, configurations, and unusual activity
- Monitors for indicators of compromise during or after maintenance
- Can trigger alerts if post-maintenance behavior is outside expected patterns

Azure AD / Entra ID

- Controls access to systems and portals during remote maintenance sessions
- Conditional Access can enforce MFA and location/device-based restrictions for admins or vendors
- Identity logs help track who accessed what, and when

Microsoft Log Analytics and Sentinel

- Ingest logs from maintenance sessions, updates, and system changes
- Provide timeline views and historical analysis for audit and compliance
- Correlate maintenance activity with potential incident detection

Summary

Maintenance might seem routine, but in cybersecurity, routine tasks are often exploited precisely because they're routine.

By applying structure, documentation, and oversight to maintenance processes, you can ensure that your systems stay secure while remaining up-to-date and functional.

When CUI is at stake, it's not enough to fix or update systems—you need to do it with discipline, visibility, and accountability.

Coming Up Next

Next, we'll explore Media Protection, the control family that focuses on securing how sensitive information is stored, transferred, and destroyed—especially on physical and removable media. You'll learn how to lock down USB drives, protect backup data, and securely dispose of devices without risking data exposure.

Let's keep the momentum going.

Control Family: Media Protection

Overview

In today's cloud-first world, we often think of data as something invisible—files in SharePoint, messages in Teams, records in databases. But data still lives on physical media too—USB drives, backup tapes, laptops, smartphones, and hard drives inside servers.

The Media Protection control family in NIST 800-171 focuses on securing how data is stored, transported, and destroyed, especially when it lives on removable or portable media. This includes physical protection, access control, encryption, labeling, and secure disposal.

This family contains four main requirements that aim to ensure:

- CUI stored on media is protected from unauthorized access
- Media is controlled during transport
- CUI is rendered unrecoverable when no longer needed
- Policies exist to guide staff in handling all types of media properly

While it may seem straightforward, improper media handling is one of the most overlooked ways sensitive information gets lost, stolen, or exposed.

Why It Matters

Media might be small, but the risks are huge.

A single lost USB stick, laptop, or smartphone could contain:

- Export-controlled design documents
- Personally identifiable information (PII)

- Sensitive contract data or pricing

- System credentials or internal configurations

If that device isn't encrypted or properly wiped, someone with basic technical skills could extract CUI from it—sometimes within minutes.

And it's not just about theft. Media can also be mishandled through:

- Insecure shipping or mailing

- Unlabeled backup drives sent offsite

- Disposal in a regular trash bin

- Using unapproved personal devices for file storage

Media Protection helps you stay ahead of these risks by introducing policies, procedures, and technologies that reduce your organization's exposure.

Common Challenges

Media protection often falls through the cracks because it operates in the physical world, where automated controls aren't always present. Here are common issues organizations face:

1. Lack of Media Control Policies

If your organization hasn't defined what kinds of media are allowed, where they can be used, or how they should be protected, users are left to make decisions on their own—which leads to inconsistency and risk.

2. Unencrypted Media

Devices like USB drives, portable SSDs, and external hard drives are frequently used without encryption—making them vulnerable if lost or stolen.

3. Insecure Media Transport

Media transported between sites (physically or electronically) may be sent without protection, tracking, or authorization—especially if handled by third parties or in emergency situations.

4. Inadequate Media Sanitization

When devices reach end-of-life, many are discarded or recycled without ensuring the data is wiped or destroyed. In some cases, data recovery is still possible—even after a "delete."

5. Use of Personal Devices

Allowing employees to store files on personal USB drives or devices increases the risk of data loss and makes it difficult to maintain control over CUI.

Example Implementation Steps

Protecting media doesn't require shutting down flexibility—it requires planning, control, and awareness. Here's a step-by-step way to align with the Media Protection controls.

Step 1: Define and Enforce a Media Handling Policy

Create a policy that defines:

- What types of media are authorized (e.g., encrypted USB drives, company laptops)

- Who can use removable storage and under what conditions

- How to request, label, store, and transport media

- What procedures must be followed when media is retired or disposed of

This policy should apply to all forms of media—electronic and non-electronic, removable and fixed.

Step 2: Require Encryption for Portable Media

Ensure that any device storing CUI is encrypted. This includes:

- USB drives
- Laptops
- External hard drives
- Backup media (such as tapes or portable storage)
- Mobile phones (if used to access or store CUI)

Use enterprise-managed tools to enforce encryption policies, such as:

- BitLocker for Windows
- FileVault for macOS
- Managed app policies for mobile devices

Where possible, prevent the use of unencrypted storage through endpoint management settings.

Step 3: Limit and Monitor Use of Removable Media

Use technical controls to limit or block USB ports and storage unless explicitly needed. Implement:

- Device control policies to prevent unauthorized drives from being used
- Logging and alerting for removable media usage
- Approval workflows for requesting access

This helps reduce "shadow storage" and ensures visibility into when and where CUI is transferred.

Step 4: Secure Media Transport

If media containing CUI must be physically transported:

- Use tamper-evident packaging and shipping labels
- Require tracking numbers or delivery confirmation
- Keep records of who transported it and when
- Avoid using personal vehicles or public transportation without safeguards

Train employees to avoid casual or insecure methods—such as mailing unencrypted devices or handing USBs across desks.

Step 5: Label Media Appropriately

Label all media containing CUI with a clear indication that it holds sensitive content and must be protected. Consider:

- "CUI" or similar marking on storage devices
- Barcode or asset tag tracking
- Owner contact information in case of loss

Unlabeled media creates confusion and increases the chance of accidental mishandling.

Step 6: Sanitize or Destroy Media Before Disposal

Before disposing of or reusing any media that stored CUI:

- Use secure wiping tools that overwrite data (not just "delete")
- Follow NIST 800-88 guidelines for media sanitization
- Maintain a log of destruction activities (who, when, how)
- For highly sensitive data, physically destroy the media (e.g., shredding, degaussing)

Never donate or sell old equipment without thoroughly validating data removal.

Microsoft / Intune / Azure / Entra M365 Alignment

Media Protection is about more than physical devices—it's about how you control and monitor data movement. Microsoft tools can help enforce these protections at the software and policy level.

Microsoft Intune

- **Removable Storage Control**: Intune configuration profiles can block or limit the use of USB ports or specific storage devices.

- **Encryption Enforcement**: Require BitLocker encryption before a device is marked as compliant.

- **Remote Wipe**: If a device is lost or stolen, use Intune to remotely wipe corporate data or the entire device.

- **Conditional Access with App Protection**: Limit CUI access only to apps that prevent copying data to unprotected storage.

Microsoft Purview (formerly Compliance Center)

- **Data Loss Prevention (DLP)**: Detect and block attempts to transfer CUI to unauthorized storage locations, including USB drives or personal cloud accounts.

- **Auto-labeling of sensitive content**: Tag documents and emails containing CUI, making them easier to track and protect.

- **Insider Risk Management**: Monitor for users attempting to copy large amounts of sensitive data to external media.

Microsoft Defender for Endpoint

- **Device Control**: Monitor or block USB drive usage on managed endpoints.

- **Anomaly Detection**: Alert when new or unusual storage devices are connected.

- **Threat Indicators**: Flag endpoints exhibiting behavior typical of data exfiltration.

Microsoft 365 and OneDrive

- **Cloud Storage Controls**: Store sensitive files in protected environments like OneDrive for Business or SharePoint instead of portable media.

- **Versioning and Retention**: Reduce the need for users to make personal backups by using cloud-based, version-controlled storage.

Summary

Media Protection is about more than preventing theft—it's about retaining control over sensitive data, even when it leaves your network.

By creating clear policies, enforcing encryption, limiting the use of removable devices, and securing disposal practices, you reduce the chance of CUI being lost, mishandled, or stolen.

With Microsoft's endpoint and compliance tools, you can implement many of these protections automatically—turning policy into practice, and securing data at every stage of its lifecycle.

Coming Up Next

In the next chapter, we'll explore Personnel Security, which focuses on vetting, monitoring, and removing user access as employees come and go.

Control Family: Personnel Security

Overview

Your systems can be patched, your firewalls can be hardened, and your devices can be encrypted—but if the wrong person has access, all of that can be bypassed.

The Personnel Security control family in NIST 800-171 focuses on managing who is trusted to access your systems and data, particularly Controlled Unclassified Information (CUI). It ensures that individuals are properly vetted before they're granted access, and that their access is promptly revoked when they leave or no longer need it.

This family contains two essential but critical requirements:

1. Screen individuals prior to authorizing access to CUI

2. Ensure system access is removed when personnel leave or no longer require it

While simple on the surface, these controls help prevent some of the most damaging and avoidable types of data breaches—those caused by insiders or former employees with lingering access.

Why It Matters

When we talk about cybersecurity, it's easy to focus on external threats. But many incidents happen because of insider risks, including:

- Disgruntled former employees who retain access to systems

- Staff members accessing data they shouldn't have

- Third-party contractors mishandling sensitive information

- Lack of background screening for users with privileged access

Personnel Security helps reduce these risks by ensuring that only trustworthy individuals are granted access to CUI—and that access is removed the moment it's no longer needed.

Even if all other technical controls are in place, failure to manage user access on the human side can render your defenses ineffective.

Common Challenges

Despite being essential, Personnel Security is often treated as an HR task and overlooked by IT and security teams. This results in several common issues:

1. Inconsistent Background Screening

Organizations may not have a formal policy for vetting employees or contractors, especially when roles evolve over time or hiring practices differ by department.

2. Delayed Access Removal

When an employee leaves, their access may remain active for days, weeks, or longer—especially if there is no automated offboarding process or centralized access control.

3. Lack of Role-Based Access Reviews

Employees accumulate access as they change roles, but those permissions are rarely reviewed or adjusted. This leads to excessive or outdated access levels.

4. Poor Communication Between HR and IT

HR may know when someone is leaving, but if that information isn't quickly shared with IT, account removal can be delayed—sometimes indefinitely.

5. No Tracking of Third-Party Personnel

Vendors, contractors, and temporary staff may have accounts or device access but aren't always tracked or offboarded as carefully as full-time employees.

Example Implementation Steps

Personnel security is as much about process and communication as it is about technology. Here's how to establish a solid foundation that aligns with the NIST 800-171 requirements.

Step 1: Establish a Screening Policy

Define a consistent policy for background checks and personnel screening. Consider:

- Requiring criminal background checks for individuals with access to CUI
- Vetting contractors and third-party support staff to the same standard as employees
- Screening personnel before granting access—not after

Document screening requirements in job descriptions and contracts, and ensure they're applied uniformly.

Step 2: Maintain a Central List of Authorized Users

Create and maintain a master list of users who are approved to access systems that store or process CUI. This should include:

- Full-time employees
- Contractors
- Temporary staff

- Interns
- Third-party vendors

Include start and end dates, roles, and what systems they're allowed to access.

Step 3: Define an Access Authorization Workflow

Before granting access, ensure:

- The request is approved by a manager
- The individual has completed any required training (e.g., security awareness)
- Background screening has been completed
- The access granted matches the job role

Avoid blanket access—grant only what's necessary, and document the approval.

Step 4: Automate the Offboarding Process

When someone leaves the organization or changes roles:

- Disable all user accounts immediately
- Collect and wipe any company-owned devices
- Reclaim ID badges, keys, or physical access tokens
- Remove access to email, cloud services, VPNs, and internal portals

Ideally, use HR system integration to automatically trigger access removal based on employee status changes.

Step 5: Audit Access Regularly

Perform periodic reviews of who has access to CUI and confirm that:

- All users still require access

- Access levels are appropriate for current roles

- No terminated users or contractors still have active accounts

Use access certification campaigns (especially in large organizations) to enforce this practice at scale.

Step 6: Include Personnel Security in Vendor Management

When working with outside service providers or vendors:

- Require that they screen their personnel to the same level you require internally

- Ensure they notify you when someone leaves or changes roles

- Limit access to only the systems and data necessary for their work

Include these expectations in service-level agreements (SLAs) and contracts.

Microsoft / Intune / Azure / Entra M365 Alignment

Microsoft tools can help streamline Personnel Security processes by tying identity and access directly to user lifecycle events.

Entra ID (Azure Active Directory)

- **Dynamic Groups**: Automatically assign users to the right groups based on department or job role.

- **Access Reviews**: Conduct recurring reviews of user access for key systems, groups, or applications.

- **Lifecycle Workflows (Premium)**: Automatically onboard and offboard users based on HR system triggers or account changes.

- **Privileged Identity Management (PIM)**: Grant just-in-time admin access with automatic expiration and approval workflows.

Microsoft Intune

- **Device Management**: Remove access and wipe company data from enrolled devices when users are deprovisioned.

- **Compliance Policies**: Block access to apps or data if a user or device falls out of compliance.

- **App Protection Policies**: Protect company data on BYOD devices, and automatically remove access when employment ends.

Microsoft Purview Compliance Center

- **Insider Risk Management**: Detect risky behavior from users who may be preparing to leave or exfiltrate data.

- **Audit Logs**: Track user activity before and after termination for incident response or investigations.

- **Data Loss Prevention (DLP)**: Block or alert when users attempt to share CUI outside approved boundaries.

Microsoft 365 Admin Center

- **User Access Management**: Quickly disable accounts, remove licenses, and revoke sign-in access.

- **License Reporting**: Identify inactive accounts or unused licenses that may represent forgotten users.

Summary

Personnel security isn't just an HR issue—it's a core part of your security strategy.

By screening users before access, ensuring timely offboarding, and performing regular access reviews, you can prevent many of the insider-related risks that lead to compliance violations and data breaches.

With the right coordination between IT, HR, and security—supported by automation and policy—you can protect your systems from human error and oversight just as effectively as you protect them from external threats.

Coming Up Next

In the next chapter, we'll explore Physical Protection, the control family focused on securing access to physical facilities, devices, and infrastructure. You'll learn how to protect CUI by limiting who can physically reach the systems that store or process it.

Let's keep going.

Control Family: Physical Protection

Overview

Cybersecurity often conjures images of firewalls, encryption, and cloud defenses—but some of the most critical risks aren't digital. They're physical.

If someone can walk into your office, plug in a USB drive, or walk out with a laptop containing CUI, no firewall in the world can stop them.

The Physical Protection control family in NIST 800-171 addresses this risk head-on. It focuses on ensuring that only authorized individuals have physical access to systems and facilities that store, process, or transmit CUI.

This control family contains six specific requirements, all designed to ensure:

- Access to sensitive areas is controlled
- Visitors are monitored and logged
- Physical barriers and protections are in place
- Systems and media are protected from physical threats and theft

Whether your CUI is stored in a data center, an office building, or a remote worker's laptop bag, physical security is essential to keeping it protected.

Why It Matters

Cybersecurity incidents don't always require hacking tools. Sometimes, all it takes is:

- A stolen laptop from a car seat

- An unescorted visitor plugging into an open network port

- An unlocked server room in a shared office space

- A janitor accidentally throwing away a printed file containing sensitive data

In many environments, CUI lives on physical systems—desktops, laptops, USB drives, printed documents—and those systems are only as secure as the rooms, buildings, and people around them.

By implementing physical protection controls, you prevent unauthorized individuals from gaining access to sensitive hardware, storage, or paper-based data, regardless of their intentions.

Common Challenges

Organizations often overlook physical security, especially in remote or hybrid work environments. Here are some common pitfalls:

1. Shared or Open Workspaces

Offices with shared spaces, flexible seating, or public meeting rooms may lack physical barriers that protect devices and documents.

2. No Access Controls to Sensitive Areas

Server rooms, network closets, or storage areas may be left unlocked, or protected only by basic door locks without monitoring.

3. No Visitor Logging or Escort Policies

Visitors may enter areas containing CUI without proper vetting, logging, or escort, making it hard to detect unauthorized presence.

4. Unattended Devices and Paper

Employees may leave laptops or printed CUI unattended in conference rooms, break areas, or vehicles, where they can be easily stolen or viewed.

5. Inconsistent Physical Security for Remote Workers

Remote employees working from home or on the road may lack basic physical security controls—like screen locks, secure storage, or destruction methods for sensitive data.

Example Implementation Steps

Strong physical protection doesn't mean turning your office into a fortress—it means managing who has access, where, when, and how. Here's how to do it effectively.

Step 1: Identify CUI-Handling Areas

Start by mapping where CUI is stored or processed physically:

- Onsite servers and endpoints
- Employee workstations and laptops
- Backup storage devices
- File cabinets and printed records
- Meeting rooms where CUI is discussed

This helps determine which areas require access controls and monitoring.

Step 2: Implement Physical Access Controls

Restrict access to sensitive areas using:

- Keycards, biometric locks, or PIN codes
- Locked doors for server rooms, storage areas, or file cabinets
- Alarm systems for after-hours access attempts
- Reception desks or checkpoints to prevent unauthorized entry

Only authorized personnel should have access, and permissions should be reviewed regularly.

Step 3: Establish Visitor Management Procedures

Create a formal visitor policy that includes:

- Visitor sign-in logs (manual or digital)
- Issuing visitor badges or passes
- Escorting visitors at all times
- Verifying ID before entry to secure areas
- Retaining logs for a defined period

Make sure staff are trained to challenge or report unescorted visitors.

Step 4: Enforce Device Security Practices

Ensure employees physically secure devices and documents by:

- Locking laptops in drawers or cabinets when unattended
- Using cable locks for desktop hardware
- Requiring screen auto-locks after a short period of inactivity
- Prohibiting the storage of CUI on personal or unmanaged devices

Train staff to never leave laptops, USB drives, or printouts containing CUI in cars or public spaces.

Step 5: Secure Equipment in Transit

When transporting laptops, USB drives, or physical records:

- Use lockable briefcases or transport containers
- Encrypt all digital storage devices

- Keep items in direct possession—never check them with luggage
- Avoid storing sensitive devices in vehicles unless absolutely necessary

Remote workers and traveling staff should receive specific guidance and training on safe transport of devices.

Step 6: Train Staff and Monitor Compliance

Educate your team on physical security expectations, including:

- Locking up when leaving for the day
- Reporting lost or stolen devices immediately
- Challenging unescorted individuals in secure areas
- Not propping open secure doors or lending badges

Conduct periodic walk-throughs and physical security audits to reinforce policy and detect issues.

Microsoft / Intune / Azure / Entra M365 Alignment

While Microsoft tools are primarily digital, they can support aspects of physical protection by extending visibility and enforcement to devices, users, and locations.

Microsoft Intune

- **Device Compliance Enforcement**: Require encryption, password protection, and screen locks on all managed devices.
- **Remote Wipe**: Erase corporate data from lost or stolen devices, including mobile phones and laptops.

- **Geolocation Policies**: Restrict access based on physical location (e.g., only allow access from known IPs or managed networks).

Entra ID (Azure Active Directory)

- **Conditional Access Based on Location**: Block access from unknown or high-risk locations, supporting physical security by narrowing approved access points.

- **Identity Logging**: Monitor and log physical sign-ins at kiosks, shared terminals, or secure workstations.

- **Privileged Access Controls**: Restrict administrative access to systems that may be physically vulnerable.

Microsoft Defender for Endpoint

- Detects abnormal user behavior that may result from unauthorized physical access (e.g., unexpected logins, odd work hours, USB device connections).

- Alerts administrators to possible data exfiltration or misuse resulting from physical compromise.

Microsoft Purview Compliance Center

- Use Data Loss Prevention (DLP) rules to prevent printing or copying of CUI to unencrypted storage, reducing the spread of sensitive data to unsecured physical formats.

- Use Insider Risk Management to flag users who suddenly access large volumes of sensitive files—potentially in preparation for physical theft or misuse.

Summary

Physical Protection may seem simple—but it's where many cybersecurity programs are weakest. All it takes is a lost laptop, an unescorted visitor, or an unlocked server room to put CUI at risk.

By controlling physical access, monitoring sensitive areas, and reinforcing secure behavior among staff, you can dramatically reduce your exposure to both accidental and malicious breaches.

Combine thoughtful policies with technology-supported enforcement, and you'll build a strong foundation for securing CUI both on-site and in the field.

Coming Up Next

In the next chapter, we'll explore Risk Assessment, where you'll learn how to identify, prioritize, and respond to cybersecurity threats within your environment—building the strategic lens that informs all other control decisions.

Let's keep moving forward.

Control Family: Risk Assessment

Overview

Every organization has limited time, budget, and personnel. You can't address every security concern at once—so how do you decide what matters most?

That's the purpose of Risk Assessment, one of the most strategic control families in NIST 800-171. This family helps you identify which threats are most relevant, what vulnerabilities exist, and where you should focus your efforts to protect CUI.

This control family includes three requirements:

1. Periodically assess the risk to organizational operations and assets
2. Scan for vulnerabilities and remediate them
3. Monitor for security alerts and updates to assess risk in near real-time

It's about building awareness and making informed decisions. Without a risk assessment process, you're operating blind—reacting instead of planning.

Why It Matters

Cybersecurity isn't just about locking things down—it's about understanding what could go wrong, how likely it is to happen, and what the impact would be if it did.

Risk assessments help you:

- Prioritize the implementation of security controls
- Allocate resources effectively

- Understand which systems are most critical

- Identify gaps in policies, technologies, or processes

- Make compliance efforts more focused and efficient

For organizations handling CUI, risk assessments ensure that your protections are not just compliant, but proportionate to the threats you face.

It also sends a clear message to partners and auditors: "We know where we're vulnerable, and we're doing something about it."

Common Challenges

Risk assessments are often misunderstood or neglected, especially in smaller organizations. Here are some typical issues:

1. Risk Assessments Aren't Performed Regularly

Many companies treat risk assessments as a one-time task, rather than a living process. But environments, threats, and technologies change—and risk must be re-evaluated.

2. Assessments Are Too Technical or Too High-Level

If the assessment is too technical, it's hard for leadership to act on. If it's too vague, IT teams won't get actionable insights. Striking the right balance is key.

3. No Link Between Risk and Controls

Identifying risks is only half the battle. Many organizations don't take the next step: mapping those risks to controls, solutions, or mitigation efforts.

4. Vulnerability Scanning Isn't Integrated

Vulnerability scans are valuable but often conducted in isolation. Without context from the broader risk environment, the results may not lead to prioritized action.

5. Risk Documentation Is Incomplete or Inaccessible

If the results of the assessment live in a spreadsheet that no one reads—
or aren't documented at all—opportunities for improvement are lost.

Example Implementation Steps

A good risk assessment doesn't need to be complex. It just needs to be
honest, structured, and repeatable. Here's how to build one that aligns
with NIST 800-171.

Step 1: Define Your Risk Assessment Process

Document how your organization conducts risk assessments, including:

- Frequency (e.g., annually or after major changes)
- Scope (systems, data, locations, departments)
- Participants (IT, security, leadership, operations)
- Methodology (qualitative, quantitative, or hybrid)

A common approach is to score risks based on likelihood and impact,
producing a simple risk rating such as:

- Low
- Medium
- High
- Critical

This framework helps teams prioritize next steps based on clear criteria.

Step 2: Identify and Catalog Assets

List all systems, applications, and devices that handle or store CUI. For
each, document:

- What kind of data it holds
- Who uses it
- Where it's located (physically or digitally)
- How it's protected

This forms the foundation for evaluating risk.

Step 3: Identify Threats and Vulnerabilities

Next, list potential threats to your assets. These could include:

- Insider threats (accidental or malicious)
- Phishing and credential theft
- Ransomware
- Data loss or corruption
- Unauthorized physical access
- Third-party/vendor risk

Then, evaluate which vulnerabilities in your systems or processes could be exploited by those threats. These might come from:

- Missing patches
- Misconfigurations
- Weak passwords
- Unsecured devices
- Lack of monitoring

Step 4: Evaluate Risk

For each asset-threat-vulnerability combination, assess:

- **Likelihood**: How probable is it that this will occur?

- **Impact**: If it happens, how serious is the effect on operations or data?

- **Current Controls**: What protections are already in place?

- **Residual Risk**: What's the risk level after existing controls are considered?

You can organize this in a risk register or matrix to prioritize actions.

Step 5: Conduct Vulnerability Scans

Use scanning tools to automatically assess systems for:

- Missing patches or outdated software

- Open ports and services

- Default credentials

- Known vulnerabilities (CVEs)

Prioritize remediation of high-severity issues, especially on systems handling CUI.

Run scans regularly—monthly is common—and always after major updates or deployments.

Step 6: Track Threat Intelligence and Security Alerts

Stay informed about new threats, vulnerabilities, and attack techniques using:

- Vendor threat bulletins (e.g., Microsoft Security Advisories)

- Government feeds (e.g., CISA, NVD)

- Security forums or ISAC groups

- Managed service provider (MSP) updates

Evaluate whether emerging threats could impact your systems, and update your risk assessment accordingly.

Step 7: Document and Act

Record your findings in a formal risk assessment report that includes:

- Top risks and their scores
- Suggested mitigation strategies
- Responsible owners and timelines
- Residual risk after mitigation

Use this document to inform decisions, justify security investments, and demonstrate compliance during audits.

Repeat the process on a set schedule and update it when systems, threats, or personnel change.

Microsoft / Intune / Azure / Entra M365 Alignment

Microsoft's tools offer robust capabilities for identifying risks, conducting vulnerability assessments, and responding to new threats—essential elements of this control family.

Microsoft Defender for Endpoint

- Performs vulnerability assessments across endpoints
- Provides risk exposure scores based on severity and prevalence
- Offers remediation guidance for detected vulnerabilities
- Integrates with threat intelligence to flag known exploit paths

Microsoft Secure Score

- Offers a real-time evaluation of your Microsoft 365 environment's security posture

- Identifies weaknesses and provides prioritized recommendations
- Tracks progress over time and maps improvement to risk reduction

Microsoft Defender Vulnerability Management (Premium)

- Provides comprehensive asset inventory and software exposure mapping
- Includes threat and vulnerability correlation based on real-world data
- Flags risky configurations and missing updates

Microsoft Sentinel

- Aggregates logs and alerts from across your environment
- Supports custom threat detection and response rules
- Correlates user, system, and application events to detect emerging risks
- Helps visualize attack paths and potential impact

Microsoft Purview Compliance Manager

- Provides compliance assessments with risk scores for NIST 800-171 and other standards
- Offers recommended actions and evidence tracking
- Links control requirements with Microsoft product features and policies

Summary

Risk Assessment is your strategy layer—the process that helps you make smart, informed decisions about where to focus your security efforts.

When you identify what matters most, where you're vulnerable, and how to respond, you gain control over your cybersecurity program rather than being controlled by it.

Risk isn't something to fear—it's something to understand and manage. NIST 800-171 doesn't expect perfection. It expects that you know your risks and are actively working to reduce them. That's the foundation of good security and smart compliance.

Coming Up Next

Next, we'll explore Security Assessment, the control family focused on reviewing and testing your existing security controls. You'll learn how to validate your policies, detect weaknesses, and use continuous improvement to strengthen your protection of CUI over time.

Let's keep going.

Control Family: Security Assessment

Overview

It's one thing to have security controls in place. It's another to know that they're working.

The Security Assessment control family in NIST 800-171 focuses on validating that your organization's security practices are not only implemented but also effective, up to date, and continuously improving.

This family includes three key requirements:

1. Develop, document, and periodically update your security assessment plan

2. Assess the effectiveness of your security controls

3. Correct identified deficiencies and update security plans accordingly

In short, this control family ensures that you're not just checking boxes—you're verifying that the boxes you've checked are actually doing their job.

Why It Matters

Security controls can degrade over time. A firewall rule might be overridden. A patch management process might fall behind. A policy might go unenforced. Without regular assessments, these issues often go unnoticed—until an incident occurs.

Security Assessment matters because:

- Environments evolve—new apps, devices, users, and threats are introduced constantly

- Controls weaken over time—through misconfiguration, staff turnover, or inattention

- Auditors and leadership need proof that what's in place is actually working

The goal isn't perfection—it's awareness and progress. A mature security program doesn't claim to be flawless. It identifies gaps, learns from them, and improves over time.

Common Challenges

Many organizations struggle with security assessments because they require time, coordination, and an honest look at what might not be working.

Here are some common challenges:

1. No Formal Security Assessment Plan

Without a documented approach, assessments become ad hoc or inconsistent. This makes it hard to compare results over time or prioritize follow-up actions.

2. Assessments Are Too Infrequent

Assessments are often done once—maybe during implementation—and never repeated. But technology and threats move fast. Controls that worked last year may no longer be effective today.

3. Focus on Paper, Not Practice

Some assessments rely solely on documentation reviews—policies, plans, checklists—but never validate actual system behavior or user practices.

4. Gaps Are Identified, but Not Addressed

Even when assessments reveal weaknesses, the findings are sometimes ignored or delayed due to lack of ownership or resources.

5. No Metrics for Success

Without defined goals or measurement standards, it's difficult to know whether the program is improving—or where it needs to.

Example Implementation Steps

A good security assessment process is repeatable, evidence-based, and action-oriented. Here's how to build and sustain one that aligns with NIST 800-171.

Step 1: Develop a Security Assessment Plan

Document a plan that defines:

- **Scope**: Which systems, controls, departments, or processes are included

- **Frequency**: Annually is a common baseline, but high-risk areas may require more frequent reviews

- **Assessment Types**:

    o **Control Reviews**: Are required policies and tools in place?

    o **Technical Testing**: Are those tools configured correctly and effective?

    o **User Behavior**: Are policies being followed in daily operations?

- **Assessment Methods**: Interviews, document reviews, technical scans, audits

- **Roles and Responsibilities**: Who conducts the assessment, who receives the report, and who's accountable for remediation

Make the plan accessible and easy to update as your organization grows.

Step 2: Evaluate Control Implementation

For each NIST 800-171 control family:

- Review documentation to verify policies exist and are current
- Examine configurations to confirm alignment with requirements
- Check for automation or enforcement (e.g., Intune device compliance, MFA enforcement)
- Interview team leads to understand real-world practices

If a control is partially implemented or not enforced, document that clearly.

Step 3: Perform Technical Testing

Use tools and processes to validate security configurations:

- Run vulnerability scans
- Test patching and update processes
- Review logs and alerting capabilities
- Check encryption status on endpoints and media
- Simulate access attempts with test accounts to verify RBAC

This moves the assessment from theory into practice—helping you catch blind spots.

Step 4: Conduct Access Reviews

Ensure access to CUI and critical systems is:

- Granted based on job role
- Reviewed periodically
- Revoked promptly when users leave

These reviews are often best done in collaboration with department leads or system owners.

Step 5: Document Findings and Remediation Actions

For every issue identified:

- Describe the finding
- Explain the risk or impact
- Assign ownership
- Define next steps and timelines for resolution
- Track progress

This creates accountability and supports both internal audits and external compliance checks.

Step 6: Use the Results to Improve

Security assessment isn't about pointing fingers—it's about driving improvement. Use the results to:

- Prioritize security initiatives
- Adjust budget and resource allocation
- Update training programs or policies
- Justify changes to leadership

Repeat the assessment process regularly and compare results over time to measure maturity.

Microsoft / Intune / Azure / Entra M365 Alignment

Microsoft provides robust tools to help you evaluate the effectiveness of your controls, detect drift, and identify areas for improvement.

Microsoft Secure Score

- Continuously assesses the security posture of your Microsoft 365 environment
- Offers prioritized improvement actions with scoring impact
- Maps recommendations to NIST 800-171 and other compliance frameworks

Microsoft Defender for Endpoint

- Provides real-time insights into device compliance, patch status, and threat exposure
- Identifies missing protections or risky configurations
- Supplies reports for ongoing assessments

Microsoft Compliance Manager (in Purview)

- Offers built-in assessments for NIST 800-171
- Tracks control implementation status, provides improvement actions, and stores evidence
- Assigns responsibility for controls and tracks progress over time

Intune and Endpoint Manager

- Reports on device compliance, configuration profiles, and application protection

- Helps assess whether policies are being enforced and devices meet baseline requirements

Entra ID (Azure Active Directory)
- Supports access reviews for groups, roles, and applications
- Logs administrative actions and user activity for audit review
- Manages conditional access policies and enforcement reporting

Microsoft Sentinel
- Aggregates logs from multiple systems
- Supports ongoing threat detection and anomaly investigation
- Provides hunting queries and rule templates to test detection capabilities

Summary

Security Assessment ensures that your controls don't just exist—they actually work.

Through planning, testing, review, and correction, you can build a security program that learns and evolves over time. That's what real security looks like—not perfection, but continuous progress.

Assessments allow you to spot weaknesses before attackers do, prove to auditors that you're serious about security, and build confidence across your organization.

Coming Up Next

In the next chapter, we'll explore System and Communications Protection, where you'll learn how to secure data in transit and at rest, segment networks, and protect against unauthorized data exposure—one of the most technical and vital parts of protecting CUI.

Let's keep going.

Control Family: System and Communications Protection

Overview

Data is constantly on the move—traveling between devices, across networks, and through applications. And wherever that data flows, threats can follow.

The System and Communications Protection control family in NIST 800-171 focuses on securing how your systems communicate, transmit, and store information—especially Controlled Unclassified Information (CUI).

This is one of the largest and most technical control families, with 16 requirements. These controls are designed to:

- Protect the confidentiality and integrity of CUI in transit and at rest

- Isolate systems to prevent unauthorized access

- Block unauthorized connections or transmissions

- Secure boundaries between networks and systems

- Control the use of publicly accessible services

Think of this family as the digital version of locking doors, closing blinds, and placing sensitive discussions behind soundproof walls. It ensures CUI doesn't leak through insecure systems or get intercepted on its way to its destination.

Why It Matters

CUI is only secure if it stays within trusted boundaries—and only flows between trusted users and systems.

But threats don't just come from malicious actors on the internet. Risks can also come from:

- Misconfigured email servers
- Unencrypted transmissions between apps
- Shadow IT services that bypass controls
- Open ports or protocols that expose internal systems

This control family matters because it ensures you're not just protecting your users and devices—you're protecting the paths that connect them.

Strong system and communication protections are essential to:

- Prevent data interception and man-in-the-middle attacks
- Protect against unauthorized data sharing or forwarding
- Limit attack surfaces on exposed services
- Isolate high-risk systems or environments

Common Challenges

Due to its technical nature, this family often introduces challenges around implementation and management. Common issues include:

1. Inconsistent Encryption Practices

Some systems may use TLS or VPNs, while others transmit data unencrypted. Without enforcement, there's no guarantee CUI is protected in transit.

2. Lack of Network Segmentation

When every system is on the same flat network, it becomes easy for threats to spread laterally. Sensitive systems aren't isolated from less critical ones.

3. Overly Permissive Firewalls or Ports

Legacy applications or poor firewall hygiene can lead to excessive open ports, exposing systems unnecessarily to internal or external threats.

4. Unmonitored Public Interfaces

Systems or services (like web apps or APIs) that are internet-facing often go unreviewed, leaving room for exposure or data leakage.

5. Unknown or Unsecured Communication Channels

Remote users may send data through personal email, unauthorized cloud tools, or messaging apps that aren't compliant with your policies.

Example Implementation Steps

Here's how to approach System and Communications Protection in a structured, practical way.

Step 1: Encrypt Data in Transit

Ensure that all communications involving CUI—between users, systems, or services—are encrypted using industry-standard protocols. This includes:

- HTTPS (TLS 1.2 or higher) for web applications and portals
- VPNs for remote access
- Encrypted email and file-sharing tools
- Secure API connections

Review all communications paths and replace any legacy or plaintext protocols (like FTP, Telnet, or HTTP) with secure alternatives.

Step 2: Encrypt Data at Rest

Data stored on servers, databases, mobile devices, and removable media should be encrypted. This includes:

- Laptops with full-disk encryption (e.g., BitLocker, FileVault)
- Cloud storage with encryption at rest
- Encrypted backups
- File- and folder-level encryption where appropriate

Ensure that encryption keys are protected and managed properly.

Step 3: Segment Your Network

Use network segmentation to isolate:

- Systems containing CUI
- Guest and contractor networks
- Administrative interfaces
- Cloud environments from internal infrastructure

Implement VLANs, firewalls, or microsegmentation tools to control communication between segments based on business need.

Step 4: Control Communications at the Boundary

Establish secure boundaries between internal systems and external networks (e.g., the internet or third-party connections). This includes:

- Firewalls that enforce allowlists
- Intrusion detection/prevention systems (IDS/IPS)

- Proxy servers or gateways for outbound traffic
- Blocking unnecessary or dangerous outbound protocols

Document what traffic is allowed through your perimeter—and why.

Step 5: Disable Unused Services and Ports

Review systems to identify open ports and services that aren't needed. Disable or remove them. Common culprits include:

- Unused remote desktop or SSH ports
- Default services that were never shut down
- Testing interfaces left enabled in production

This reduces your attack surface significantly.

Step 6: Monitor for Unauthorized Transmission

Implement tools to monitor and block unauthorized attempts to:

- Send CUI to personal email
- Upload sensitive files to external storage (e.g., Dropbox)
- Connect to unapproved cloud services
- Transfer files using unsanctioned apps

Use Data Loss Prevention (DLP) policies to alert or block on detection.

Step 7: Secure Public-Facing Services

For systems that must be exposed to the internet (e.g., portals, public APIs, or customer apps):

- Enforce strong authentication (MFA, SSO)
- Perform regular vulnerability scans and patching

- Use Web Application Firewalls (WAFs)

- Limit access using IP filtering or Conditional Access

- Disable directory listing or verbose error messages

These safeguards reduce exposure and prevent information disclosure.

Step 8: Review and Log Communications

Track how systems communicate, including:

- Logs of user access and file sharing

- API calls between applications

- External connections to cloud services

- VPN and remote access logs

Monitor for anomalies and retain logs for incident response and audits.

Microsoft / Intune / Azure / Entra M365 Alignment

Microsoft tools offer a wide range of options for protecting system and communication channels—especially in hybrid and cloud-first environments.

Microsoft Intune

- **Configuration Profiles**: Enforce encryption settings on all devices.

- **Compliance Policies**: Block access from devices that are not encrypted or fail to meet security baselines.

- **App Protection Policies**: Prevent corporate data from being copied or transmitted through unauthorized channels.

Microsoft Purview

- **Data Loss Prevention (DLP)**: Monitor and block sensitive information from being sent via email, Teams, SharePoint, or to USB drives or cloud apps.

- **Information Protection**: Apply encryption and access restrictions to labeled content.

- **Activity Explorer**: Review how sensitive data is being used, shared, and stored.

Microsoft Defender for Endpoint

- Detects and blocks unauthorized connections or suspicious network activity

- Identifies insecure configurations and open ports

- Maps lateral movement attempts within your environment

Microsoft Sentinel

- Correlates communications logs from across endpoints, servers, and cloud services

- Provides visibility into system-level data flows and external communications

- Alerts you when network or application behavior falls outside expected patterns

Microsoft Azure

- Azure Firewall and Network Security Groups (NSGs) for controlling traffic flow between resources

- Azure Bastion for secure remote access to VMs without exposing RDP/SSH to the internet

- Private Link for restricting data communication to private network paths instead of public internet

Entra ID (Azure AD)

- **Conditional Access**: Restrict access based on user location, device state, or app sensitivity

- **Authentication Logging**: Track user sign-ins, token usage, and session behavior

- **Secure Hybrid Access**: Control external system access through federation or identity integration

Summary

System and Communications Protection ensures your security program extends beyond users and devices to the data itself—how it flows, where it lives, and who can access it.

By encrypting transmissions and storage, isolating networks, controlling communications, and securing public-facing services, you protect CUI against interception, misuse, and loss.

While this family is one of the most technical in the framework, it's also one of the most powerful when properly implemented. And with the right tools and strategy, it becomes manageable—even for smaller teams.

Coming Up Next

In the next chapter, we'll cover System and Information Integrity—the family focused on keeping your systems healthy, up-to-date, and protected from malware and tampering. You'll learn how to monitor for threats, apply patches, and detect unauthorized changes before they become major problems.

Control Family: System and Information Integrity

Overview

Even the best security defenses can't prevent every vulnerability or issue. Systems break. Updates fail. Malware evolves. Users make mistakes.

The System and Information Integrity control family in NIST 800-171 helps you address this reality head-on by ensuring your organization can detect, respond to, and recover from issues affecting system performance, security, and trustworthiness.

This family includes seven requirements that focus on:

- Detecting and addressing flaws (like bugs or misconfigurations)
- Identifying and mitigating malicious code
- Monitoring for security alerts
- Taking corrective action when unauthorized changes or anomalies occur

In short, this control family is about keeping your systems clean, healthy, and resilient—so that CUI remains protected, even when things go wrong.

Why It Matters

Think of your IT environment like a car. Even if you lock the doors and use a GPS tracker, it still needs regular oil changes, tire checks, and brake inspections to remain safe.

Similarly, your systems need regular maintenance, updates, and monitoring to:

- Stay protected against newly discovered vulnerabilities

- Detect early signs of compromise or malfunction

- Respond quickly when something unexpected occurs

- Prevent small problems from becoming major security events

System and Information Integrity ensures that you notice when something's wrong and have a plan to fix it—before it leads to data loss, exposure, or operational disruption.

Common Challenges

Many organizations struggle with this family because it requires continuous attention and proactive maintenance. Here are common issues:

1. Delayed Patch Management

Systems often remain unpatched for weeks or months after vulnerabilities are disclosed, leaving them open to exploitation.

2. Lack of Antivirus or Endpoint Protection

Not all endpoints have standardized protection in place—or the protection isn't monitored, updated, or enforced centrally.

3. No Real-Time Monitoring

If logs and alerts aren't reviewed, threats can go unnoticed for long periods. Small issues grow into large incidents before anyone is aware.

4. Users Ignore Warnings

Security warnings, pop-ups, and prompts may be dismissed or bypassed by users without escalation or follow-up.

5. Inconsistent Remediation Processes

When issues are detected, organizations sometimes fail to act quickly, or actions aren't well-documented or coordinated.

Example Implementation Steps

System and Information Integrity is about establishing systems and processes that detect and respond to issues early and effectively. Here's how to get started:

Step 1: Implement Endpoint Protection

Install and enforce antivirus/antimalware software on all endpoints that handle CUI. Ensure:

- Real-time scanning is enabled

- Definitions are updated regularly (automatically)

- Logs are retained and reviewed

- Centralized management is used to monitor health and compliance

Microsoft Defender for Endpoint, CrowdStrike, or similar enterprise-grade tools can fulfill this requirement.

Step 2: Establish a Patch Management Process

Define and document how updates are applied to:

- Operating systems

- Third-party applications

- Network equipment and appliances

Patch cycles should be:

- Timely (within a defined window after updates are released)

- Documented (what was updated, when, and why)

- Prioritized (high-severity vulnerabilities addressed first)

- Tested (in staging environments if possible)

Use tools like Windows Update for Business, Intune, or SCCM to automate and manage patching.

Step 3: Monitor and Respond to Security Alerts

Monitor alerts from:

- Endpoint protection tools
- SIEM platforms (like Microsoft Sentinel)
- Threat intelligence feeds (e.g., CISA, MSRC)
- Cloud platforms (Microsoft 365 Defender, Azure Security Center)

Assign a person or team to regularly review and respond to alerts. Define escalation procedures and document actions taken.

Step 4: Prevent and Detect Unauthorized Code Execution

To reduce malware and rogue app risk:

- Block unauthorized scripts and executables using AppLocker or Windows Defender Application Control (WDAC)
- Prevent installation of unauthorized software
- Monitor for unusual behavior (e.g., sudden system resource spikes, unexpected network activity)

Train users to report suspicious system behavior instead of ignoring it.

Step 5: Use Integrity Checking Tools

Set up tools that monitor for unauthorized or unexpected changes to critical files or system settings. Examples include:

- File integrity monitoring (FIM)
- Registry change detection

- Configuration drift tools

Automated alerts should notify the appropriate team when unauthorized changes occur.

Step 6: Define a Remediation Workflow

When a flaw or issue is detected, your response should be:

- Documented: Describe the issue, affected systems, and impact

- Assigned: Designate an owner for resolution

- Tracked: Use a ticketing system to follow the issue through to completion

- Reviewed: Conduct a post-remediation analysis to ensure resolution and prevent recurrence

Include remediation timelines based on risk severity (e.g., critical flaws addressed within 24 hours).

Step 7: Train Users to Report Issues

Your users are often the first line of defense. Teach them to:

- Report unusual system behavior or security pop-ups

- Avoid ignoring antivirus warnings

- Use official support channels—not coworkers—for resolving suspicious issues

Include real-world examples in training so users understand what to watch for.

Microsoft / Intune / Azure / Entra M365 Alignment

Microsoft provides a rich ecosystem of tools for maintaining system integrity and proactively managing threats.

Microsoft Defender for Endpoint

- Real-time malware detection and remediation
- Behavioral analysis to detect fileless attacks and zero-day exploits
- Automated investigation and response (AIR) features
- Integration with Microsoft Sentinel for deeper threat correlation

Microsoft Intune

- Enforces patch management through Update Rings and configuration profiles
- Monitors compliance for endpoint health, antivirus status, and OS version
- Supports app control policies to block unauthorized software

Microsoft Secure Score and Compliance Manager

- Track configuration settings and endpoint protection coverage
- Identify misconfigurations and control gaps
- Offer step-by-step remediation guidance for improving security posture

Microsoft Sentinel

- Ingests system logs, security alerts, and audit trails

- Detects anomalies and potential threats across endpoints and cloud resources

- Supports automated playbooks for remediation and alert escalation

Windows Security Baselines

- Pre-configured settings for security hardening

- Includes recommendations for Defender AV, firewall settings, and script restrictions

- Easily deployable through Group Policy or Intune

Summary

System and Information Integrity is about being proactive instead of reactive. It ensures your systems are monitored, maintained, and protected—not just once, but continuously.

With these controls in place, you don't just defend against threats—you build a resilient environment that can detect issues early, respond effectively, and bounce back quickly.

For organizations managing CUI, this means fewer surprises, faster recovery, and stronger compliance.

Coming Up Next

In the final chapter of this book, we'll tie it all together with a practical roadmap for implementing NIST 800-171, helping you move from knowledge to action. You'll learn how to prioritize your efforts, document your progress, and prepare for compliance reviews with confidence.

Implementing NIST 800-171 – A Practical Roadmap

Overview

By now, you've explored every control family in NIST 800-171. You understand the intent behind the standard, the specific protections it requires, and how tools—especially from Microsoft—can support those efforts.

But knowledge alone doesn't lead to compliance. You need a plan.

This final chapter brings everything together by outlining a practical, step-by-step roadmap to help your organization implement NIST 800-171 successfully and sustainably. Whether you're starting from scratch or tightening up an existing program, this roadmap will guide you from assessment to action—and through continuous improvement.

Why This Matters

NIST 800-171 isn't just a cybersecurity checklist. It's a structured framework for protecting Controlled Unclassified Information (CUI) in non-federal systems. Compliance is often required for:

- Government contracts (especially DoD-related work)
- CMMC (Cybersecurity Maturity Model Certification)
- Defense industrial base and supply chain partnerships

Failure to comply could mean:

- Loss of contract eligibility
- Breach of data handling agreements
- Exposure of sensitive data

- Regulatory or reputational risk

More importantly, implementing this framework gives you a robust, tested foundation for cybersecurity—one that protects your organization and its partners.

Step-by-Step Roadmap

Let's walk through the full process of implementing NIST 800-171, broken down into actionable phases.

Phase 1: Preparation and Discovery

Objective: Understand your environment and determine the scope of the project.

Key Actions:

- Identify what qualifies as CUI in your organization
- Map where that CUI is stored, processed, or transmitted
- Identify systems, people, and workflows that interact with CUI
- Determine whether you are handling CUI directly or supporting others who do

Deliverables:

- Asset inventory (devices, users, data repositories)
- System boundary definition
- Initial data flow diagram

Phase 2: Gap Assessment

Objective: Compare your current security controls to NIST 800-171 requirements.

Key Actions:

- Review all 14 control families (110 controls in total)
- Determine whether each control is:
  - Fully implemented
  - Partially implemented
  - Not implemented
- Document the current state and supporting evidence

Tools to Help:

- Microsoft Compliance Manager's NIST 800-171 assessment
- Internal or third-party gap analysis templates

Deliverables:

- Gap analysis report
- Compliance score or maturity baseline

Phase 3: Plan of Action and Milestones (POA&M)

Objective: Create a prioritized plan for addressing gaps.

Key Actions:

- Assign ownership to each control
- Estimate effort and time required for remediation
- Determine dependencies, tools, and required approvals
- Define milestones and success criteria

Deliverables:

- A formal POA&M document, often required for contract compliance
- Updated risk register (for controls not implemented immediately)

Phase 4: Remediation and Implementation

Objective: Fix the gaps and implement missing or weak controls.

Key Actions:

- Deploy policies and technical controls across systems
- Configure Microsoft 365, Intune, Defender, and Entra to align with requirements
- Train users on new processes or tools (MFA, DLP, incident reporting, etc.)
- Document each implemented control and the evidence of compliance

Common Priorities:

- Enforcing MFA across all users and admins
- Encrypting all devices with BitLocker/FileVault
- Controlling access to CUI repositories
- Enabling audit logging and alerting
- Segmenting networks or cloud workspaces

Deliverables:

- Updated system security plan (SSP)
- Control implementation records
- Evidence collection (e.g., screenshots, logs, policy files)

Phase 5: Testing and Validation

Objective: Make sure your controls are working as expected.

Key Actions:

- Conduct internal audits or third-party validation
- Perform vulnerability scans and penetration tests

- Run tabletop exercises for incident response
- Verify system hardening and endpoint protection

Deliverables:

- Security assessment report
- Updated documentation and remediation tickets
- Metrics or dashboards showing compliance trends

Phase 6: Ongoing Monitoring and Maintenance

Objective: Keep your environment compliant and secure over time.

Key Actions:

- Schedule recurring access reviews and system audits
- Patch systems regularly and log change control
- Monitor Microsoft Secure Score and Intune compliance posture
- Stay current with evolving CUI definitions and NIST updates
- Update your POA&M and SSP as changes occur

Deliverables:

- Continuous compliance dashboard or report
- Updated policies and procedures
- Audit log retention and response playbooks

Best Practices for Success

To make your NIST 800-171 program more effective, keep these best practices in mind:

- **Make it a team effort.** Involve HR, IT, security, compliance, and leadership. Everyone has a role to play.

- **Automate what you can.** Use Microsoft tools like Intune, Defender, and Purview to reduce manual work and ensure consistency.

- **Keep documentation up to date.** Your SSP and POA&M are living documents—not static files.

- **Use maturity as your mindset.** Compliance is the minimum. Security maturity is the goal.

- **Prepare for CMMC.** NIST 800-171 is foundational for CMMC Level 2. Get ahead now to avoid future contract disruption.

Microsoft Tools That Power Your Roadmap

Throughout this book, we've highlighted how Microsoft's security ecosystem can streamline your path to NIST 800-171 compliance:

Control Area	Microsoft Tools
Identity & Access	Entra ID, Conditional Access, MFA, Privileged Identity Management
Device Protection	Intune, Defender for Endpoint, Compliance Policies, Encryption Enforcement
Data Protection	Microsoft Purview, Sensitivity Labels, DLP, Information Barriers
Logging & Monitoring	Microsoft Sentinel, Defender XDR, Secure Score, Audit Logs
Vulnerability Management	Defender for Endpoint, Microsoft Secure Score, Microsoft Defender Vulnerability Management
Documentation & Compliance	Microsoft Compliance Manager, Purview Compliance Portal

These tools don't just help you check boxes—they help you build a sustainable, well-integrated security architecture.

Summary

Implementing NIST 800-171 isn't about chasing compliance for the sake of a contract. It's about building trust—trust with your customers, your partners, and the government agencies you work with.

It's about proving that your organization takes data protection seriously, and that you've done the work to manage risk, prevent incidents, and respond effectively when challenges arise.

With a structured roadmap, the right tools, and a culture of continuous improvement, you can meet the requirements of NIST 800-171—and create a more secure, resilient organization in the process.

What's Next

This book was written to make the complex, technical world of cybersecurity compliance more approachable. You've now got the knowledge, the strategy, and the tools. The next step is execution.

If you're looking for support:

- Start with a gap assessment using Microsoft Compliance Manager.

- Explore the other books in this series for deep dives into Microsoft Purview, Intune, and more.

- Take advantage of training through Olympus Academy or your internal learning platforms.

- Or work with a trusted advisor to help plan and accelerate your implementation.

Remember—every step you take builds a stronger foundation. Keep going.

www.ingramcontent.com/pod-product-compliance
Lightning Source LLC
LaVergne TN
LVHW022349060326
832902LV00022B/4337